Tristan da Cunha

Wartime Invasion

ALLAN B. CRAWFORD M.B.E.

GEORGE MANN PUBLICATIONS

Published by
George Mann Publications
Easton, Winchester,
Hampshire SO21 1ES
01962 779944

Copyright © Allan Crawford 2004
Copyright © George Mann Publications 2004

Cover illustration by Roy Wilkinson

All rights reserved.
No part of this publication may
be reproduced, stored in a retrieval
system, or transmitted in any form or
by any means, electronic, mechanical,
photocopying, recording or otherwise,
without the prior permission
of the copyright holders.

A CIP catalogue record for this book
is available from the British Library

ISBN 0954629914

Other titles by this author:

I went to Tristan
(Hodder & Stoughton 1941)

Tristan da Cunha and the Roaring Forties
(Charles Skilton / David Philip 1982, 0284985899)

The Tristan Times
(published as a limited edition, 1943)

Penguins, Potatoes and Postage Stamps
(Anthony Nelson, 1999, 0904614689)

George Mann Publications

photo: A.B.C.

This book is dedicated to the memory of

Arthur and Martha Rogers

whom I first met in 1937 and whose philosophies of life,

both of this world and the next, often return to my thoughts.

I spent over three and a half years of blissful residence

in their old home, shown above, between 1942 and 1948.

Illustrations

Acknowledgements

Having reached the time in life when one is largely dependent on one's friends for help, this section is one of great importance to the author.

I sincerely thank Robin Taylor of Solihull and Mike Faulds of Dalkeith for their voluntary work on my sixty year old manuscript and George Mann of Winchester, all three of whom are responsible for its publication.

I also thank my son Jamie, who lives with me, Ron Burn of Bromley, Guy Marriott of Bourne End, Mike Mueller of West Virginia and my older son, Martin, and his family of Cape Town whose continued encouragement has been essential for success.

Closer to my home in Wadhurst are kind visitors who often call in to offer help, amongst whom are: Rosalie, David and Betty; Miriam, Peter and Janet; Bryan, Ivan and Maureen; Tina, Christine and Penny. Liz, my dentist, also helped on several occasions with bulky laminations of collages for the Island Museum and Craft Shop and Liz's Australian friend, Sally, who waded through several hundred colour slides to find the picture of Arthur and Martha Rogers for the dedication page.

Lastly, but by no means least, I thank all my friends in our Tristan da Cunha Association, especially Michael Swales, our Honorary Secretary and Treasurer for over seventeen years of dedicated work, and our much-loved Island-born Chairman, Lorna Lavarello-Smith, whose parents and grandparents I knew long before she was born!

4

Contents

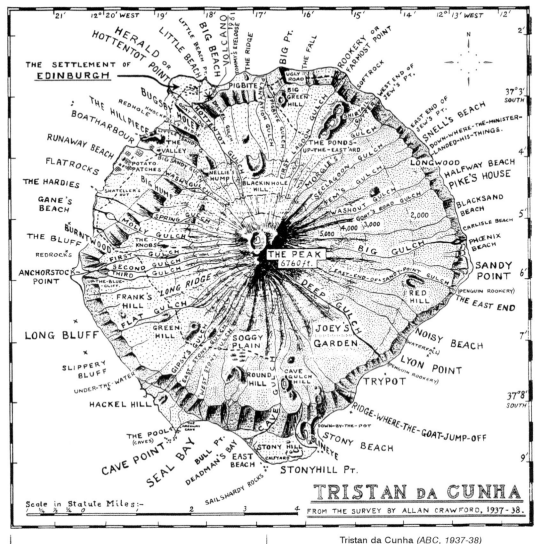

Tristan da Cunha (ABC, 1937-38)

Nightingale Island, twenty-five miles from Tristan da Cunha. (ABC 1940)

Archway Cave at Cave Point, Tristan da Cunha
(ABC 1940)

Foreword

Allan Crawford's fourth book, *Tristan da Cunha: Wartime Invasion*, portrays the small community living on the island of Tristan da Cunha in the middle of the South Atlantic Ocean.

In 1937, as an apprenticed engineer in his early twenties, Allan volunteered as a surveyor for a Norwegian Scientific Expedition and drew the first detailed map of the islands. Later, he published his adventures in his first book, *I went to Tristan*.

Four years later, Allan joined up for war service as a meteorologist and accompanied the Royal Navy on its 'invasion' of Tristan to establish a listening post for enemy submarines. It was five years later, while still in uniform and waiting to be demobilised, that Allan first wrote the manuscript that forms the basis of this present book. It was not published at the time because he became involved in his civilian occupation as a marine meteorologist in Cape Town, his marriage and a family. The manuscript was shelved and forgotten for almost sixty years!

Having returned to England with his wife in 1977, Allan researched the history of the island in his retirement. This resulted in the publication five years later of *Tristan da Cunha and the Roaring Forties*.

Further research for the design of stamps for Tristan's post office inspired Allan's third beautifully illustrated book in 1999, entitled *Penguins, Potatoes and Postage Stamps*.

This latest book is a unique account of the reaction of the people of Tristan da Cunha to the modern world – the introduction of money, postage stamps and the British Administration. Originally written in 1946, it vividly brings to life the individuals, families and community of that time. The Christian faith held by many of the islanders, and shared by Allan, has been an important factor in keeping the community together through all these changes.

Allan is Life President and a founder member of the Tristan da Cunha Association. In 2002, aged 90, he deservedly received from the Queen the award of the MBE for his devoted services to the people of Tristan.

David Payne
Wadhurst, East Sussex

Prologue

Having noticed the spate of books and TV programmes produced since the turn of the Millennium on the subject of World War II, many backed by reminiscences from aged witnesses, it seemed appropriate that I, now in my 92nd year, should throw in my lot before it is too late.

In 1942, at the age of 30, I was employed in Pretoria as a wartime reserve engineer where Naval Intelligence located me to assist in their planned invasion of Tristan da Cunha, the loneliest inhabited island in the world in the middle of the South Atlantic Ocean. Their purpose was to acquire a base on the island which would help the Allied forces with information vital for our cause and I was the only known person in Africa with local knowledge of conditions on the island. I was enlisted into the South African Air Force Meteorological Section, the expedition comprising Army, Naval and Air Force personnel embarked on the Armed Merchant Cruiser, *H.M.S. Dunnottar Castle*, based in Simonstown.

This was to be the second naval invasion, the first taking place in 1816, involving one of the original settlers, Corporal William Glass, a Scot from Kelso, who was a gunner. This was also organised from the Cape of Good Hope, to claim the island in the name of the Crown to prevent it being used by the French to organise the escape of Napoleon Bonaparte from St. Helena, on which island he was incarcerated by the British for the rest of his life.

The opportunities of my involvement struck me at once as I realised that I would witness a complete metamorphosis on the island. I knew that, of the one hundred and eighty nine souls on the island, only seven had been in the 'outside world' and had seen a horse and cart or experienced fresh water emerging from a tap! I therefore armed myself with both still and movie cameras, pens, paper and notebooks, for I knew I was destined to spend many more months there.

Towards the end of W.W.II, back in South Africa waiting to be demobilised, I was posted to carry out meteorological observations from Maun, in the middle of Bechuanaland, now Botswana, which ironically enough seemed more remote from civilisation than Tristan da Cunha, for there was nothing to do in the evenings! However, I was armed with my portable typewriter, paper and notes so I spent the evenings preparing the manuscript of this book but because of paper and other shortages in Europe caused by the war, few books were presented for publication and my manuscript was filed away to await better days.

At that stage of my life on a voyage from Southampton to Cape Town I met a girl who became my wife and, with the arrival of two sons and a very interesting job in the weather bureau as a maritime meteorologist, I thought no more about my manuscript residing in the loft! I had returned to the U.K. on pension and written an historical book on Tristan, without any reference to the manuscript lurking now on the back shelf of a cupboard, until I received correspondence one day from a friend, Robin Taylor, who had come across during his research, a letter written by me in 1949 to Mr John Butler in which I mentioned the manuscript. After searching my loft I unearthed the manuscript. Robin Taylor and my son, Jamie, decided that it should have a more productive fate than the municipal dustbin, especially as its contents written 60 years ago recorded special adventures.

I hope that I have captured and conveyed the pleasure, enjoyment and inherent fascination of my special wartime adventure on 'the loneliest island in the world'.

Allan Crawford

March 2004
Wadhurst, East Sussex

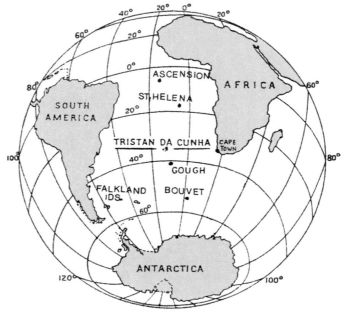

The Brink of Adventure

In the European winter of 1937 I left the bleak weather of the northern hemisphere for the sunshine of South Africa. I was, at the time of departure not bound by any contract and was free to do as I chose. The chance meeting of Dr Erling Christophersen, Curator of the Botanical Museum, based in Oslo, Norway, while sailing south added greatly to the interest of the voyage, for his personality and companionship were qualifications worthy of acquaintance.

One day he informed me that he was bound for Tristan da Cunha, where he was leading a party of a dozen fellow Norwegians on an expedition to study the various branches of science in which they were interested. When he mentioned that he did not have a surveyor, I jokingly volunteered and, to my amazement, he took me seriously. And so, giving up all other ideas of work in South Africa, I sailed from Cape Town in 1937 for the island of Tristan da Cunha, 1,700 miles west of the Cape of Good Hope.

The 1937-38 Norwegian Scientific Expedition to Tristan da Cunha in Cape Town before departure. The leader, Dr Erling Christophersen is third left, front row and the author is on the right, back row.

We were stationed in Tristan da Cunha for four months. During that time we were all ably assisted by one hundred and eighty nine islanders, whose co-operation, enthusiasm and hard work enabled us to record all the information required to write up research papers and even to give lectures. A popular book on the experience of the expedition as a whole was published by Dr Christophersen in three languages, and I, in the capacity of surveyor, drew charts and published my own account in book form of our adventure. Indeed it was a great satisfaction to me to learn that the British Admiralty, replaced their charts of Tristan da Cunha with mine!

In March 1938 I returned to the Cape and proceeded to Johannesburg where I made an abortive attempt to settle down. After three months in one of the best engineering firms in the city my inherent wanderlust prompted me to leave faster than I had arrived and a few weeks later I was the guest of a kindhearted captain of the Royal Navy. After an interesting five weeks calling at Luderitz, Monrovia (Liberia), Dakar and the Cape Verde Islands, where I climbed to the peak thinking once more that I was on Tristan, we arrived at Portsmouth during one of the coldest spells for a number of years.

I had come home to England to see my parents and to write a book. After a pleasant Christmas in Cornwall I went up to London to write, because I was fully convinced that if I was having to pay for a lodging without any return, thus I should get the book written all the quicker and then be ready for my next move. I handed in my manuscript which was returned after two agonizing weeks of waiting with a note that it was 'unsuitable for publication as the manuscript stands'. I really thought that my world was ending. It was only the encouraging letter from a very old lady, Mrs Barrow, the wife of a missionary who had herself spent three years on Tristan da Cunha between 1906 and 1909, that I realised there was more to come.

Things were at a low ebb and it was obvious that I had to get some sort of work once more. But behind all these dark clouds, both international and personal, I could see two extremely good results of my return visit to England. My visit to my parents in Cornwall was most opportune in that I was able to help my father. In London I met one of the nicest and most useful men it could ever have been my wish to meet, and the man to whom in years to come I would be so much indebted for his advice and interest, General Sir Reginald Wingate.

With the knowledge that my visit to London had been fruitful in spite of the fact that my book was as yet unpublished, I returned, at my own expense, to South Africa. With cash running low and no guarantee of work of any description, I was not going to be particular about the type of work I undertook, so long as

I was able to earn a living.

On the 3 September 1939, war was declared. By 4 o'clock, after purchasing extra editions of the local Sunday newspapers to make sure that war had really broken out, I sent a telegram from the G.P.O. telegraph office in Johannesburg volunteering my services, in any capacity, with the Naval authorities in Simonstown.

This time, however, it was not so easy to break with the present state of things, and although I received a telegram in reply informing me that my name and details had been put down on their lists, the creation of 'key men' in engineering works in the South African heavy industries prevented any further attempts of leaving for any other adventures. Here again I saw plans arranged for me in the most satisfactory manner by that power we sometimes call Fate, but which may well be the hand of the Almighty.

A friend, Anne Hills, expressed the desire to read the manuscript of my book in order to see why it was not suitable for publication as it stood and possibly do something towards getting it corrected. Then followed several months of intensive work for both of us, alongside our ordinary, routine and individual daytime jobs.

Several months elapsed and renewed efforts to join up were all in vain. After my arrival in Pretoria to join the steelworks, I thought it would be a good idea to reside in an Afrikaans boarding house so that I could learn this dialect of Dutch spoken in South Africa, a dialect which can be of the utmost value when trips out into the bushveld and country were necessary. It was therefore in a losieshuis, or lodge house, that I spent the next year.

One incident in connection with this sojourn is worthy of record which reflects greatly to the credit of the C.I.D. of the Union, for they were forever on the look out for any 'fifth column' agents.

Rewriting my book in the evening often entailed late hours and many a night my typewriter was working overtime until after midnight. This went on for some weeks and, being of an independent nature, I did not venture to discuss my private affairs with my fellow boarders. One night, just as my typewriter had got into its 'tik-tik' mode once more, I heard a knock at my door. I opened it to see who should be calling at this hour, when a youth carrying a briefcase invited himself into the room. It did not take him long to enter into conversation.

"My name is van der Westhuizen, and I come from the C.I.D.," he began, placing his brief case on the table, "and reports have come from here that you are engaged in secret work. I have come from police headquarters to see what you are up to!"

When war broke out in Europe, the position in South Africa was not so clear as in England as regards the country's loyalties. There were a large number of Germans in this country and some, of Dutch extraction, had not forgotten the Anglo-Boer War of some forty years ago. Everyone therefore was on the lookout and suspicious movements were at once reported by the trustworthy to the local police. Some member of the community to which I had attached myself was proving more British than the British, and my exclusion to my room every night to write my book was too good an opportunity for him to miss. Needless to say I showed van der Westhuizen my manuscript on my table and an Admiralty chart on the wall with my name engraved on it as surveyor; he departed with a fusillade of apologies for troubling me under circumstances that had been quite misleading and false.

Eventually Anne and my efforts were rewarded and a cablegram from my agents in London brought the good news of its publication. I had great satisfaction, while on a stroll one day in Pretoria, when I saw several copies on sale in a bookseller's window and I realised that my work, my Tristan da Cunha interlude, was completed. I was then prepared to call this episode of my life a thing of the past and never thought that I should ever visit the island again.

With my book on sale and a slight knowledge of Afrikaans, I moved from my losieshuis to the congenial company of friends in one of the most pleasant suburbs of Pretoria. With my inherited desire to be on the move, if only in the same small town, I decided to move to a private hotel. With all my worldly belongings packed in the back of my small motor car, I transferred myself a few miles nearer town in the beautiful surroundings of the famous Union Buildings, Pretoria, the seat of the Government during the bleak Cape winter months.

Three nights after this unexpected move I entered into a secret conversation, over the fire in the lounge of a private hotel, with Lieutenant Smith R.N.V.R.

"Are you by any chance the fellow called Crawford who has been to Tristan da Cunha?" he enquired.

"I am," I replied.

"Well, this is a great secret and you are naturally not expected to ask any questions but I have a letter from Commander Bishop of Simonstown asking me if I could trace a fellow by that name who has been to Tristan. It really is extraordinary that we should meet like this."

"Well, it is all the more extraordinary because four days ago I never entertained the prospect of moving from my friends in Waterkloof where I was so happy for over a year. Commander Bishop is a very good friend of mine, if it is Commander W A Bishop, but isn't he in England?"

Smith confirmed that it was W A Bishop alright, commonly known as 'Bish', and it was interesting enough to hear about an old friend without what was to follow.

"The letter I have received wishes me to trace you, and to get a report from you, if you will be so good as to give us one, on the landing possibilities on Nightingale Island, near Tristan da Cunha, in the South Atlantic Ocean," Smith continued.

"I've never been to Nightingale," I told him, adding, "but I know quite a lot about the island from hearsay and know two things for certain, namely that there is no fresh water on the island and that there are no beaches. Landings must be made up a perpendicular rock some five feet high out of the water."

"Right, now if you could write all you know in the nature of a report, I shall forward it down to Simonstown and we shall be very pleased," Smith concluded.

That was as far as the conversation went in connection with the South Atlantic, and, with a 'that's all very interesting', I knew the time had come for silence and the topic changed.

Nevertheless, my state of mind became restless and when I went to bed that night I conjured the most interesting and adventurous possibilities in my mind. Could this be a chance to join up, was this the unknown opportunity for which I had been waiting? This was going to be interesting, I thought, as I started to put two and two together. It seemed to me obvious that, if a meteorological officer was interested in the middle of the South Atlantic Ocean, it was very likely that there was a plan in the air for the establishment of a meteorological station on that island. Here was perhaps an opportunity for me, for I was one of the only people in Africa who knew anything about these islands. I therefore drafted the following letter to Commander Bishop whom I had known for several years:

Pretoria, Oct 1941

Dear Commander Bishop,

I hope that the report on the island proved valuable to you. Please do not worry I have already forgotten all that I surmised as the result of a Met. Officer making enquires about the island, and of course have not breathed a word to anyone.

However, is there any chance of me joining the Met. Section and going there? I would not mind in what capacity I went etc. Anyway if there is no possibility of my joining, I would like to join the Met. Section of the Navy and go anywhere, failing that, I am a mechanical engineer and with the following qualifications would be pleased once more at having a shot at getting into the Navy. A dockyard job as a last resort.

Yours sincerely,
Allan Crawford

I had to wait nearly three weeks before I got a reply and, as it usually only took a few days for a letter to reach the Cape from the Transvaal, I rightly guessed that he had been away by sea to give the island under consideration what they call the 'once over'. October 20th brought me an interesting reply to my letter.

Office of Flag-Officer-in-Charge, Simonstown, Cape Province
16 October 1941

Dear Crawford,

Very nice to hear from you and a thousand thanks for your book which we are reading with the greatest pleasure, thank you also for the other information you sent me via Smith, which is most useful. Re your enquiry, I am afraid there is no chance now or in the near future of entering the Met. Service as an officer as I am not allowed to enter any more locally at present; but I think we may possibly be able to take you in the R.N.V.R. branch either for an appointment out here or for preliminary training in England. Failing that we may have a job in the dockyard. If this suits you, will you please make a formal application to the Fleet Officer-in-charge for a commission in the (E) Branch of the R.N.V.R. giving full particulars... etc. etc.

If on the other hand you are keen enough on the other business not to worry about a commission it is possible that Colonel Sellick might be able to take you in as an N.C.O. in the S.A.A.F. Met. Service. He has been hoping to establish a station for some time and one never knows whether it might come off some time, in which case I should think you would be the very man for him. Smith will give you an introduction. My wife reciprocates your kind wishes... etc. Perhaps I'll be seeing you.

Yours sincerely,
W A Bishop

I spent another sleepless night. I wondered what kind of a person this Colonel Sellick might be and what would be his reactions to the interview Lieutenant Smith had arranged. Eventually it turned out that my cogitations had been unnecessary for one could not have wished to meet a more pleasant and sympathetic personality.

Colonel Sellick, who was then the Deputy Director of Meteorological Services for the Union Government, shortly to be promoted to Director until the end of the war in 1945, agreed to take me on into his section either as a pupil to sit for a commission as he was short of some officers or as a corporal to go to Tristan da Cunha. He had, he said, a staff of only three persons to man the proposed station in the middle of the South Atlantic and he had already chosen the man who was to be in charge, a Flight/Sergeant.

But here again, as in the case of the offer from Simonstown, I realised that there was one job for which I was cut out irrespective of rank and one job alone for which I had the right qualifications which few others possessed. I was the only person in Africa who had spent more than two or three days on Tristan da Cunha. Of course, Tristan islanders and their offspring who settled in the Cape forty years ago were still alive and well but they were now old men and had not recently visited their old homestead. I should more correctly have said that I was the only person who knew the present two hundred islanders well.

There followed the usual exchange of correspondence, but the urgency of the matter expedited it and red tape was thrown into the waste paper basket. By 1 November 1941, I had to report to the South African Air Force Meteorological Headquarters in Pretoria and was signed on for duty. I was now an Air Mechanic by rank, which is the lowest possible and corresponded with the rank of Private in the British Army.

As I had not the slightest knowledge of meteorology except for having read the thermometers daily for the headmaster at my prep school in England, it was necessary that I spend a few months studying this, to me, a new science. At the same time, with my knowledge of Tristan da Cunha and of 'expeditions', I had other more unusual work to perform such as making out lists of equipment, advice as to the packing of stores suitable for landing.

At Port Elizabeth, or P.E. as it was called, I spent three months at the aerodrome. As soon as I arrived there, I was conscious of having been born, so it appeared, under a lucky star, for everyone whom I met in connection with my work there were extremely pleasant personalities. Captain Jack Hattle, Forecasting Officer in charge at Port Elizabeth was no exception and was the man destined to accompany me and who was to be in charge of the meteorological side of the building of the establishment there. Placed on his staff for three months, he had the job of instructing me in all matters in connection with meteorology, but at the same time I was completely free of normal routine duties although I used to help out the female staff of three W.A.A.F. personnel, as occasion demanded. At this stage discipline demanded my addressing Captain Hattle as 'sir', but afterwards he was to become one of my greatest friends.

One day I was walking along the Main Street in Port Elizabeth when I noticed my book prominently displayed for sale in a news-seller's. No-one except Captain Hattle, and later Lieutenant Kidd when he went away on leave, knew that I had ever written a book and had the fact been discovered, especially as the book was entitled *I Went to Tristan,* by perhaps one of the W.A.A.F.s at the office, the cat may have leapt out of the bag and they would have assumed the obvious, that I was destined for my second voyage to that remote island outpost. I was therefore obliged to jeopardise my sales and asked the manager if he would not mind, for military reasons, withdrawing my book from its favourable position in his shop window to the back of one of his shelves.

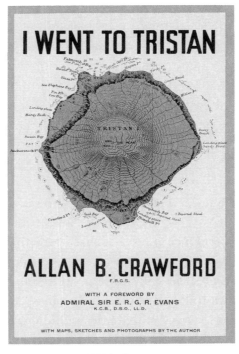

1940 leaflet

Transfer to Simonstown

I did not stay long in Port Elizabeth after the turn of the year, my destination now was Simonstown and the Royal Naval Station situated just inside False Bay on the Indian Ocean side of the Cape Peninsula. I knew Simonstown well, and being only 30 miles from Cape Town itself, I was not lost there for I had many friends in the vicinity. The time for departure was drawing near and I was needed to help Commander Bishop in the making out of lists and ordering of materials and also to learn co-operation between the Naval and the S.A.A.F. side of meteorology. He kindly met me at the station and I was taken up to the sailors' camp 700 feet up on the top of the hill above the town, known as Klaver Camp.

It was here that the naval meteorological station was situated, Commander Bishop being the Chief Naval Met. Officer (C.N.M.O.) and Lieutenant Coventry, the Forecasting Officer. Once more I realised how fortunate I was in having such pleasant and agreeable companions, for as an Air Mechanic and at the same time almost a raw recruit, they might so well have ignored me and left me to fend for myself. I was billeted in the wireless mess amongst the sailors, and from the 'detail', which was my military description at Port Elizabeth with the Navy, I became a 'hand'.

I was very puzzled at the different nomenclature upon my arrival in a sailors' mess. The floor was dubbed the 'deck' and, instead of going off duty into Cape Town, they spoke of 'going ashore'. Nevertheless, during the next three months it did not take me long to get into the run of things and I realised that the fellows amongst whom I was mixing were the backbone of the British Navy.

The day after my arrival, it was decided to hold a meeting down in the C.N.M.O.'s room of the Admiral's office. Here I found great activity in connection with H.M.S. 'Job 9' as the scheme was called, so that only those directly concerned with the project should know where the new station was to be built. I met Doreen Greg, a civilian architect who had been taken on to design the station, and one of the first rather alarming things I noticed when I studied her plans was that the dozen or so houses which constituted the living quarters of the proposed station had been drawn slap in the middle of the Island cemetery! I was proud to notice that the Admiralty Chart No 1769 which they were using was taken from my survey of 1938 but was of a small scale and the cemetery was not shown. I told Commander Bishop that in Pretoria I possessed a good plane-table survey of the Settlement and, almost as soon as I had arrived at Simonstown, I found myself with an urgent military booking once more in the train bound for Pretoria to retrieve it. The urgency with which they treated the matter prompted them to book my return the following day by plane and the trip, which otherwise would have meant a train journey of 1000 miles, was accomplished in just over four hours.

It was most pleasant to become a member of the little community of men and women, representing the Navy, Army, Air Force and civilian interests which Commander Bishop with his masterful powers of co-operation had gathered around him. Few will realise the amount of work such an important post involved. It was only such a man with tact, and at the same time a general knowledge of all the different sections with which he had to deal, who could have achieved such work in so short a time.

During my last two months in the Cape, prior to departure, it was necessary to make trips up to Pretoria on several other occasions. A shuffle in staff at the headquarters necessitated changes in plans, and I was eventually given three stripes and a crown and put in charge of the S.A.A.F. men who were to work at this new station. We called for volunteers from other members of the section and from those who volunteered to go anywhere irrespective of conditions, I chose two excellent fellows, Corporal D G Hudson and Corporal H J Heighway, to become my companions and helpers and to complete the necessary staff for this unusual job. The former, Hudson, was a Durban boy and the latter from South Africa's famous diamond centre, Kimberley. The three of us therefore assembled all the meteorological equipment we should need for at least two years and everything from the large anemometer down to the smallest drawing pin was packed into watertight boxes and labelled and numbered. At one stage, I found all the thermometers in one box and the first principle demanded that everything should be split up as the possibility of losing crates either in the docks at Cape Town, in the ship or into the sea when we were off-loading at the island itself, was a major consideration of our plans. So everything was split up as best as possible. Important boxes were covered with thin iron plate and soldered so that if they became wet or fell into the sea, they would remain dry and float.

Each of us had to get together our own special collection of interests. We might be on Tristan, for all we knew, for two years and that length of time on a small island demanded special considerations of its own. We had a large bundle of books, but those worth reading would not last for long. We had our work to do throughout the day, but that did not last until the evening. In the end most of us decided to let the problems solve themselves when we arrived at the island.

Humphrey Heighway, was a high-brow, both in literature and music, and was not to be separated from his Bach, Beethoven and Brahms. Fortunately for him, his records arrived at the island in just as good a condition as they left Kimberley. I cannot remember what Doug Hudson decided to take, for he was more of a happy-go-lucky type of fellow who could make himself at home no matter where he pitched up.

Early on, however, I conceived the idea of producing a weekly newspaper and included a duplicating machine and many reams of foolscap paper especially for the purpose. All three of us were interested in photography and so loaded ourselves up not only with our own cameras and film, but as much official stuff as we could get, for there might be special clouds in that part of the world to record. We also had our own developing equipment.

I had recently decided that cinematography was a hobby well worth the trouble of being loaded with the necessary equipment, for on film, a story could be written which cannot be recorded so graphically in any other way. The popular model of cine and its black and white film were soon traded in for a well-built Bell and Howell with 3,000 feet of colour film. I knew of the metamorphosis about to take place in the lives of the Tristan islanders.

For my part I was returning to visit old friends. With the exception of a couple of missionaries who were still alive and in England, I was the only Englishman they knew and I had plans for making a much more thorough sociological study of the people to whom I had become so attached during my presence as a member of the Norwegian Scientific Expedition. During the greater part of those four months in 1937-38, I had been engaged in surveying on the island's 6,760 ft. mountain slopes, so there was still much to be learnt from these people. They had lived in contentment and happiness for some 120 years without any major crime at all, despite the fact that they had no parliament or laws. I did not doubt that I should be fully occupied throughout my stay and, even at this stage, I had plans for living in a family home.

During one of my many visits to Pretoria, if fate had been a little kinder, I should have been in Cape Town during the few days that my father was passing through on his way from India to England. I had not seen him for three years and I had planned to get him off the ship to find work in the Cape. His only ambition at the time, he informed me later by letter, was to return to our home in Cornwall.

My departure once more to Simonstown brought me back to the song of the sea and I was soon at home with my nautical friends. As an engineer by profession I was sent to a firm in Cape Town to examine the large diesel engines that were to equip our island power station. The 2,000 pound loads that the machines weighed gave me a sickening headache when I thought of the difficulties of off-loading them without derricks or even a wharf or jetty. There were no sheltered bays or harbours at Tristan, I told them, and I was sure they would never be able to man-handle such heavy loads out of small rowing boats onto a sandy beach. But I had not bargained for the versatility of the thirty five South African Army Engineers who were to build the station.

In the event of anything untoward happening, I had to study the construction of these monsters and spent several days in the workshops watching them being taken to pieces and re-assembled.

To place a community of people on a island where very little will grow apart from potatoes and where fresh meat cannot be obtained from the local community, required special consideration with regard to diet. Being interested in this subject, I was given the task of making out the expedition's balanced diet, so I spent many weeks working out the quantities of carbohydrates, proteins and fats that each person needed in order to live in the best of health. But it did not end here. Vitamins, not to forget minerals such as salt, iron and calcium, had to be present in our daily diet in sufficient quantities to prevent scurvy, beri-beri and other ailments caused by their absence.

We also went ahead and ordered vast quantities of food, for it was not known how often, if ever, they would be able to send ships to replenish our stocks. The war outlook was at the time not good and shipping off the Cape was beginning to be in danger, so our stocks of everything were as large as we dare make them without financial embarrassment to the Admiralty.

Obtaining permission, even for the Naval authorities, to build a meteorological and wireless station on Tristan da Cunha was not easy as Tristan came under the jurisdiction of the British Colonial Office in London and in some ways its administration was an interesting experiment and the subject of close observation, given the perfect harmony that existed within a community which was mostly self-supporting and with a complete lack of any government or laws.

Without any government officials such as a magistrate, customs, postal or trade representatives the island was looking after itself well, albeit causing a little embarrassment now and again when they ran out of sugar and suchlike. The Society for the Propagation of the Gospel (S.P.G.) in London, however, and the Tristan da Cunha Fund in London (Sir Irving Gane) and Cape Town (Mr P A Snell) looked after their interests in those respects and occasional ships' visits were always preceded by appeals for necessities, supported usually well by philanthropic persons in many places of the world.

There were other considerations: there was no money on Tristan. The islanders had got along very well without this trouble-making commodity, and all exchange was carried out both externally with passing ships and internally amongst themselves by barter. A model boat was worth a suit of clothes or a pair of shoes and a day's work on the island was worth three meals from the employer throughout the day.

One of the first conditions laid down was that the 'invading' party or parties should be self-contained units in themselves and should be dependent on the islanders for nothing whatsoever. We had therefore to take enough food to last a year or two and a supply of vegetable seeds was considered good policy. We also had to be quite independent insofar as accommodation was concerned. Nothing was to be left to chance and an ample supply of tents had to be carried as the inhabitants had their own housing problems. It was quite a business to build a house when the materials were dependent upon driftwood of suitable dimensions being washed up onto the island shores.

A naval doctor would accompany the party and remain at the island, rendering his services free of charge not only to the strangers, but to the islanders too in case of necessity. He would be the senior man on the island and would have magisterial powers invested in him by the British Government. A naval padre, representing both the sailors and the civilian interests would be supplied by the S.P.G. if it was possible to find a suitable volunteer.

The placing of single men for a year or two on the island was another problem which the authorities had to face, for human nature being what it is, the lack of female companionship might result in marrying into the local island population. This was not regarded as a good idea because the strangers might remain and population of the island was already considered far more than desirable. In principal, therefore, the sailors were married men and accompanied by their wives and families. This was an excellent move but increased the work of building the station by at least double. The fact that women were to be included and catered for caused Commander Bishop no end of headaches and I remember one report proposed in the strongest of terms that, if it was not too late, they should be excluded as their presence in so confined a space on a small island might lead to problems. They would form into cliques and anyone excluded would have no possibility of a friend with whom to discuss her private affairs until after her return to the 'outside world'. It may have been wrong, but in any case it was too late.

There was another condition laid down by the authorities in the strongest of terms. The position on the island with regard to their religion was unknown at that time and nothing was to be allowed to aggravate the situation as we knew that the islanders had belonged to the Anglican Church en-bloc for over 100 years and an unfortunate misunderstanding a few years previously had upset them a little and caused a schism.

This broadly speaking was the main basis upon which we were to carry out what lay before us. With the prospects of foul weather, lack of landing facilities and the island's terrible isolation, we had much with which to occupy our minds in those early days of planning. It was quite clear from the start that South Africa and the waters around her coasts were the chief beneficiaries of a meteorological station on this island 1,700 miles to the west. Britain as a major war power with millions of tons of shipping rounding the Cape annually was not altogether a disinterested party. It was agreed that expenditure should be divided. The South African Government, through the medium of the Union Defence Force, was to supply engineers to build the station and was also to supply all the materials. They would likewise have to be responsible for the feeding of the engineers just as long as they were on the island and would also supply the three meteorologists from the South African Air Force and all of the meteorological equipment.

The United Kingdom Government, on the other hand, who would arrange for feeding the permanent party, would be solely responsible for keeping the island supplied, and would allow the visitors free quarters and furniture for the whole of their stay on the island. The buildings were to be rent free. In connection with staff, the British Government undertook to supply all wireless personnel to operate the transmitters and a doctor whose services would be free and would be placed in charge of the whole party and would have magisterial powers.

A mad, last minute, rush took place in Simonstown as the magnitude of the work in hand grew. Commander Bishop, in spite of his almost super-human capacities for work, could absorb no more, so Lieutenant Greg, assisted by Ableseaman Tooley were called in to organize the control of stores in Cape Town docks. Mrs Stella Bishop, our friendly O.C.'s civilian wife, was also recruited onto the Admiral's staff to help and Dorette Hughes made a most efficient secretary. These were the people with whom I came into contact and there were probably many others just as much involved, but they could not have been busier than our little bunch.

At Klaver Camp Lieutenants Coventry and Torrence helped me in the selection of a suitable code for the use of transmitting our weather reports when we arrived at Tristan. This code had eventually to be approved by our own O.C. Colonel Sellick in Pretoria.

It was now March 1942 and a lot of activity had been going on in other directions, quite apart from my naval friends. I made the acquaintance of Captain Sayers who was to be responsible for the construction of the buildings, and Captain N Roberts, S.A.E.C., the surveyor. Both men had made several trips to Simonstown from Pretoria and the latter had a party of thirty five South African Engineers encamped on the shores of False Bay undergoing a course in elementary seamanship.

These men, mostly recruited from the Johannesburg gold mines, were learning to row and navigate whaleboats, rig up derricks and make landings through the surf in the vicinity of 'Froggy Pond', their camp. Amongst them were carpenters, blacksmiths, tinsmiths, builders and other necessary staff such as a quartermaster. They were a fine collection of hard working fellows. The dangers they went through later on in wrestling with the furious elements of the region of the 'Roaring Forties' were due for high praise.

On 19 March 1942, we received a false alarm to embark. I was up in Pretoria and my old friend Captain Hattle in Port Elizabeth. We were telexed to arrive in Cape Town not later than the 23rd, and after Captain King handed over to me the codes and ciphers that we would use, I caught the Cape Town train once more with most of my belongings. At the same time Captain Hattle was experiencing his own mad rush from Port Elizabeth. In South Africa distances were great and to travel by train takes the greater part of a day, the journey from Port Elizabeth to Cape Town, Durban or even East London which is only 300 miles away all take at least a day and a night.

It was nice to see Jack Hattle again but we both felt pangs of disappointment when we were told that the ship could not sail for at least a week and we both returned to our home towns. Eventually, on the 27 March, we again received telexes telling us to report this time to Simonstown forthwith, and on the 29th I went up to Klaver Camp to pack all my remaining goods and chattels, this time for the last time. Commander Bishop, who was busier than ever, had spent the last few days almost incessantly on the road between Simonstown and Cape Town docks. Tooley and the South African Engineers' quartermaster were fully occupied checking the preliminary survey party's stores on board the Armed Merchant Cruiser, *A.M.C. Dunnottar Castle* (15,000 tons).

Motor vessel Dunnottar Castle, before conversion to an armed merchant cruiser for the Royal Navy.

It had been decided that the bulk of the stores for building the station should leave in May, whereas Captain Roberts with his thirty five engineers, P.O. Tel. 'Tubby' Brinkworth, Jack Hattle and I should form an advance party and land a month earlier, during which time we would be able to reconnoitre, build roads, erect temporary quarters and, if possible, erect an emergency wireless station. Another item of our equipment which we noticed as soon as we got on board was our livestock, consisting of two cows and a bull, a flock of sheep, several pigs, hens, ducks, geese, and a few goats. This unusual cargo, plus coops, pens, and enclosures of all descriptions were distributed here and there all over the decks of the ship.

During all this hum-drum of excitement and industry, Commander Bishop offered to take me and my worldly possessions from Simonstown to Cape Town, a journey which for me amounted to a glorified twenty-five mile taxi drive, for it was a question of picking me up on my doorstep and dropping me at the bottom of the gangway. I had naturally accumulated quite a large collection of baggage, since I was also taking with me as many old clothes and shoes that I could get hold of to give to the needy Tristan Islanders.

I revelled in my capacity as a meteorologist: it was amazing what independence it could give you, especially when it came to those types of duties that one always wished to avoid. But it was with great joy and expectation that I 'fell in' with the engineers on the decks of our large transport as we steamed out between the quay on either side of the entrance to Cape Town docks. We were not allowed to blow the siren, but as we stood there, all togged out in our newly acquired British battle-dress we could plainly recognise a small group at the west entrance waving us God speed.

Commander Bishop, Lieutenants Greg and Tooley were the only ones who could be recognised of the half dozen or so who alone in the world were allowed into the secret of our destination. We were on the brink of an unusual type of adventure, we were virtually on an Expedition. On board the *Dunnottar Castle,* I was at once in the prime of my enjoyment, with plenty of room all around for our party consisting of less than forty souls who were the sole occupants of this large liner, chartered especially for the voyage. Why we were so well looked after, and in wartime too, I could never make out, but I suppose she was the only ship available and capable of the 1,700 mile journey from Cape Town to Tristan at the time, and of course she had to return too.

Although we slept on mattresses spread on the floor in a deck clearing, we were moderately well housed and the ship rolled but little. We were not in convoy, but had a few guns mounted on the deck of the ship and we steered a course due west out into the middle of the South Atlantic Ocean.

We were soon used to our new surroundings. Some of the engineers, as landlubbers from the Rand, had never been to sea before and Jack, during the first day, took to his bunk. I was not so unfortunate on this occasion and it was not long before I found the bridge, the chart room and the captain's quarters. These were my first goals aboard a ship, for an intimate knowledge of the brain of the ship, in my opinion, completes that atmosphere which is essentially typical of the occasion, and Captain Bunbury was not to hinder my interest.

In fact, Captain Roberts, Jack Hattle and I were soon accepted into his confidence and asked to his cabin for drinks. We discussed everything we knew, or thought we knew, about Tristan, especially with regard to the difficulties of landing there. Tentative plans were drawn up for our course of action should we arrive and find the enemy in occupation of the island and the possibility of a mine-field surrounding the beds of kelp off the Settlement also gave us cause for thought. Jack and I offered to walk overland from the south of the island, when we would ask the islanders if they knew if the normal approaches to Big and Little Beaches were safe, but eventually we dismissed the likelihood of danger and planned to approach the island in the normal way.

My chart, I saw, was in use by the navigator and it was good to think that as a result of the Norwegian Scientific Expedition of 1937-38, we had done something of a direct contribution and value to the Empire. Without up-to-date maps of the island the possibility existed that the scheme might not have come off. With them and with the knowledge that the coastline bore a direct resemblance to the actual island, it instilled confidence in the event of anything untoward happening. Armed with maps with the local nomenclature we would always be able to find our way about.

Every three hours we took meteorological observations for record purposes, I played about in my off-hours with my newly acquired movie camera and Sgt. Hudson fed his large family of livestock. Captain Roberts decided to make a raft, and two or three days out of Cape Town his boys were busy constructing one out of drums, beams and planking what was to become *S.A.E.C. Hopeful,* destined to bear the heaviest loads ashore.

The soldiers had not been let into the secret of our destination until we were 24 hours from the Cape. Captain Bunbury broke the secret and discussed landing difficulties on the ship's radio loudspeaker system. He said that as the island was seldom visited there were no facilities for carrying out the type of landings which we were called upon to do and that we would have to be resourceful with everyone being called upon to assist no matter what his trade, profession or calling. Thick beds of kelp surrounded the island which made boating difficult.

There were no bays, and it is possible that we would have to hang around the island for a number of days before we would be able to land.

As the only member on board who had ever been to Tristan before, I was in great demand not only with the captain but also on the bridge, for the navigator had several points for discussion. Ordinary seafaring matters gradually gave place to general discussions about the islanders, how they lived and what they did.

Six days out of Cape Town, on Sunday, 5 April, I was asked to speak to the whole ship's company and let them know something about the island. I was therefore conducted to a small booth, resembling a telephone box, on the bridge, the microphone placed in my hands and I was asked to get on with it. Thirty minutes into my talk I was interrupted by a quiet knock at the door of my little box. I opened the door and saw Captain Bunbury indicating that I should place my hand over the microphone so that what he had to say should not be heard all over the ship, for the broadcast system had groups of soldiers and sailors listening everywhere.

"Just a minute," I said before I covered the mike.

The Captain, pointing, said, "The island is just coming into view now, tell them before you close down, that if they look approximately ten degrees on the port bow, they will see the island just coming into view through the haze on the horizon."

This was a wonderful end to my little talk, and after repeating the Captain's words, I went to the rail to join in the mad rush of excitement which followed this grand piece of news.

For the second time in my life I was visiting Tristan da Cunha, the most lonely inhabited island in the whole world, and the people, all of whom I knew well, did not know that an old friend was to visit them again. They have seldom seen the same face twice. Great excitement prevailed on board as during the next three hours we got nearer to the isolated place that was to be our home for the next few months. I was destined to remain the next eighteen months there, although I did not know it at the time.

The 6,760ft (2,060m) peak of Tristan da Cunha, seen from 8 miles north of the island.

It was apparent that we were arriving with fine weather and, as the island became more and more distinct the nearer we approached, the chances of landing became more and more hopeful. I took some movies from a distance of several miles and was fortunate enough to get the island under ideal conditions; one might visit Tristan a dozen times and find it dull or rainy every time.

As we steamed along the northern coast I could not resist pointing out the landmarks I knew so well and the beaches along which, four years previously, I had traversed in order to make my survey. I pointed out the Peak which I had just explained in the broadcast, was free of cloud that day.

As the houses situated on their little 'shelf' came into view, we saw six island boats with about ten to fourteen men in each, making their way out to us, bobbing up and down in the swell as they slowly neared our ocean monster. They had no idea that we were a friendly ship until we hoisted the white ensign and gave the 'V' sign blast on our siren.

The beach was possible and that thought caused the Captain and Roberts to sigh relief, for we should not have to hang about for a few days seeing that they were able to launch their boats.

Our peaceful invasion into which the Islanders were about to be plunged was to be the start of a new era, precipitated by war some three years earlier. They did not know that their lives would be turned topsy-turvy and that they would be undertaking duties and hardships of which they had never dreamt, just as we had experienced three years ago.

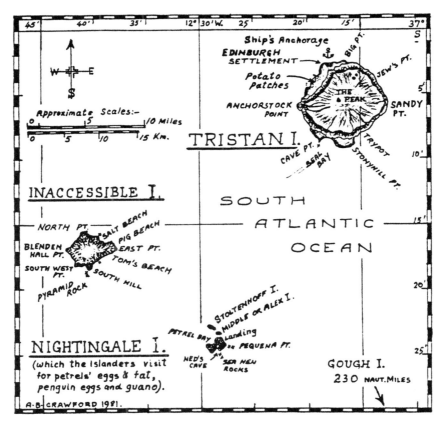

The Tristan da Cunha group of islands.

'Job 9': The Outsiders Invade

Everyone in the *Dunnottar Castle* was keyed up in anticipation of setting foot on the world's loneliest island and I had the feeling that I was returning home.

It was a beautiful day and it was obvious we should be lucky with the off-loading if everything went according to plan. As the little island boats approached, Captain Bunbury formed an impromptu reception committee consisting of himself, Captain Roberts, Captain Hattle, Sgt/Maj. Bowles and myself, and I think his No. 1, Lt. Com. Laws, was also included. Before he left the Cape the Captain had been given a declaration to read to the Head Islander as from the British Government placing before him, in but a few words, the object of our visit and asking for the island's full co-operation. Plans would have to be made in conjunction with the islanders with regard to boating the stores ashore, but the strangers at first thought they would only be needed for off-loading on the beach. Here I could not but express in the strongest terms how valuable I considered the islanders would be boating our stuff ashore, for we surely could not equal these men in operations in their own waters to which they were very well used, whereas we had never been to the island before.

It was decided that as soon as the boats came up alongside. I should take charge of proceedings and get five or six men together with their Chief, Mr. William Repetto. They would join us for discussions and the Captain was to give them tea.

We hove-to just opposite the Settlement about a mile from the shore in about twenty fathoms but we did not drop anchor for some considerable time. Presently, as the six boats came within hailing distance, the men all stood as with one accord and raised their caps in 'three cheers'. As we returned the compliment and the men drifted closer and they were not sure what to do. I gradually started to recognise first one and then the other, for they had been good companions of mine and all helped me with my work almost exactly four years previously. I think Arthur Rogers was the first I recognised for he had been my best friend and helped me most during my last stay on the island.

I had decided, and fortunately obtained the approval of Jack and Captain Roberts, that instead of living with the soldiers in their tents I would ask Arthur and Martha Rogers if I could stay with them in their island home. Comparatively wealthy and clean, as well as both being most pleasant and agreeable folk, Arthur and Martha were aged in their mid-forties, but their marriage some twenty years ago had not been blessed with children. I therefore knew that if they would have me I would be of little inconvenience and besides the last thing I wanted to do was to stay in a camp. That, I reckoned, I could do at any other time in my life in the 'outside world', but when again would I get the opportunity of living under the friendly thatch of an island home? If I made close contact with these people I should not only be able to make a close sociological survey of the islanders, but I should also be able to act my part better as 'liaison officer' between the military and the civilian population. I could help both sides, islander and soldier, and I was so keen to accomplish this that I had determined to ask Arthur as soon as he came on board.

I leaned over the rail with the boats below bobbing up and down like corks and looked for Willie. I suddenly saw that I had been recognised when quite a way off and although silence reigned below, a few islanders were excitedly pointing me out to one another, for these people have seldom seen the same strange face twice. One boat was obviously the most important and started to come up alongside the companionway which had already been lowered.

"Hello Chief," I shouted and his boat all doffed their caps and waved their welcome.

'Mr Crawford!' 'There's Crawford' and 'Please to see you' were some of the quiet replies which issued from the boat of my former acquaintances. I shouted down to Willie that we wanted him to bring up four or five men on board for a little talk.

As everybody craned over the rail to study these interesting looking men, all dressed in an odd selection of clothing ranging from naval, military and civilian with an equal assortment of hats and caps. Willie soon had his men on board and I was pleased once again to shake hands with him, his brothers Arthur and Joe Repetto, John the Baptist Lavarello, Ned Green and my old friend Arthur Rogers. I introduced the 'Chief' to the Captain and as he arranged his papers and led his little party to a secluded area on the deck I got Arthur and Willie aside and told them that the soldiers were coming ashore and they mustn't worry. They wouldn't do any harm!

A steward arrived with a tray with ten cups of tea, and Captain Bunbury asked Chief if they were all well and whether they had good crops of potatoes.

I got Arthur aside and asked after Martha and all the rest of his family. Everyone, it appeared, was well and they had seen no enemy shipping.

I more or less left them all to the Captain at this stage, for being of a retiring nature I did not like to thrust too far into the limelight. I considered my job for the time was done, although I hung around close to Arthur waiting for an opportunity to ask him if I could stay with him. Captain Bunbury read the British Government's declaration and he explained in simple language the object of our visit which, briefly, was to build a meteorological and a wireless station.

"Such things are necessary in time of war," he explained.

"Yes, Sar, sure they's necessary, an' the men will be only too please to help," Chief replied.

The islanders seemed genuinely pleased to see us and it was not long before we could see that they did not like standing about and were anxious to get on. I placed my enthusiastic proposal to Arthur and slightly had the wind taken out of my sails when he informed me that although he would be 'only too please', he would have to ask Martha. This delay kept me on edge for the next hour or two but I had the feeling that just such a request would not be turned down. Arthur said he'd send a note ashore and as the ship's whaleboats were lowered and off-loading started, I introduced him to Jack and asked him if he would help us to collect our things.

The islanders were at first told to keep their boats near the beach and when it was obvious that they would have to help in the boating too, it was arranged that gear should be trans-shipped near the kelp and the men take it ashore from there. A few soldiers went ashore, and the island women, who as was customary had come down to the beach dressed in their Easter Sunday best, were a little nervous to see soldiers bearing rifles. Some women, we heard, clutched the arms of their braver companions whereas one or two others dodged behind big boulders for safety!

"Some of the h'island women," they said, "were real skeer'd when them soldiers come ashore, for they was afraid they was going to shoot someone."

After an hour or so I was getting very anxious to get ashore for it was already four o'clock and I did not fancy spending the night on board. At that rate I might never get ashore and my inherent impatience soon came to the fore as I organised a whaleboat for our service. Jack, Arthur and I lowered all our private possessions and some of our instruments over the side of the ship into the boat. By this time we were anchored and the off-loading had been proceeding at quite a pace. But we were still a mile from the shore, and the Captain thought it unsafe to approach any nearer. Jack with a glass barograph in one hand and hanging on for dear life with the other went over the side and I followed with a barometer and my valuable movie camera slung over my shoulder. As we approached the kelp we made straight for an island canvas boat which seemed to be waiting for something to do and the familiar faces of the Tristanites radiated once more to smiles.

I discovered afterwards that when Jack and I left the ship a signal went ashore that 'Mr Crawford' was coming too, and the women did me the great honour of all returning to the beach to welcome us. I also remember eventually that I had sent a parcel to the island some years ago of a dozen bright red head-handkerchiefs, which the recipients had carefully stored away in their sea chests for special occasions! When they heard who was returning, they had donned their presents in recognition.

When we were but a few yards off, the surf, which although not rough, broke on Big Beach in long lines of white foam. I shall never forget as long as I live the picture before me. My heart missed a beat as I realised that I was returning to a community of people whom I loved and amongst whom I had many friends; I wanted to film this my life's most impressive moment, but although the camera was slung round my neck in anticipation of such good 'shots', I could do nothing, for the moment was too sacred. As the boat hit the beach and islanders gave me and Jack a helping hand forward. I leapt onto the beach and set foot on the world's loneliest island for the second time in my life. We had arrived safely and now it remained to get our cargo ashore as easily as we had come.

As I walked up the sand to greet the familiar faces, I was presented with the most extraordinary sight. Lily Glass, whom I knew well from my first visit to the island, was the first to step forward to shake my hand, and in her arms she held a large child aged about 18 months.

"Whose is this?" I asked her.

"It's my daughter, Joan," she said proudly, her face blushing.

From Lily to Alice, Alice to Kathlene and so on I went down the line from left to right, and each one of the girls we had known as single girls, during the Norwegian Expedition some four years ago, had all got married and all proudly produced their firstborn to the beach to greet us. Lily was now Lily Rogers, for she had married Arthur's brother, Victor, and my heart was sore for a moment when I thought that the girls with whom we had had such joking fun and dances were now all tied up and occupied with families of their own. I did not know the growing generation of children so well, but I soon continued with the large job of greeting some fifty women.

I found that although I remembered well every face, I could not place the names, so decided to keep silent on that score unless I was perfectly certain.

"We's please to see you, sar", each said in welcome.

"I feel that I am coming home," I said to each reply and they were very pleased.

When I got to Martha, I asked her if Arthur 'had said anything,' for I did not quite know how to broach the question of my staying with them.

"Yes, Mr Crawford, that'll be quite all right. We'll be very please to see you up at the house just when you feel like coming. We's very please to see you an' thank God you all arrive safely. We's seeing some strange things on Tristan with all them soldiers what come ashore, an' they say they's more to come."

"Thank you very much, Martha, I hope you don't mind if I send my things up to the house right away. I know they'll be safe. Yes, Martha, there are about thirty five engineers altogether, but I don't think they will all come ashore to-day."

Mrs Repetto, the head island woman and Martha's mother, was not on the beach, for Martha gave her apology and mentioned that the walk down 'allus make her half-winded' and she 'bin down h'already once, so if you care to call at the house she will be please to give you a cup of tea'.

I walked on past the jumble of cases, sacks and boxes, which were already starting to accumulate on the beach, onto the plateau towards the Settlement. Below, on the right, a party of half a dozen Sappers were already erecting tents for the night on Little Beach Point. Here Jack left me to share his tent with Captain Roberts and I walked up to Martha's house with a string of boys carrying some of my more valuable possessions.

The Settlement seemed quite unchanged with its forty little thatched houses. Walking is tough on Tristan where there were no proper roads. When I arrived up at the house to find Martha had preceded me, I collapsed into a chair in the kitchen and uttered a sigh of relief. Arthur was still busy in the boats, and did not turn up until later on towards five or six o'clock, but in the meanwhile Martha boiled a 'drop o' drink' and finished putting the final touches to my room, which was to be their 'outside room' and best in the house. I did not know it at the time, but I was destined to sleep on that bed for the next eighteen months almost without a break and the manner in which both Arthur and Martha looked after me throughout that period was as though I had been their own son, long lost and returned after a number of years in a foreign land.

I knew Arthur's house well, for during the time I had lived on the island with the Norwegians in 1937 I had often called on them and had tea. Martha left no stone unturned in order that I should be comfortable in my new surroundings.

'Did I take two pillows?' 'Would I like three or four blankets?' 'Would I like a cup of milk beside my bed and didn't I think the window should be shut because of the draught?' were but a few of the questions she placed for answer. I know that, after we had stopped talking in the friendly atmosphere of their kitchen fire at half past one in the morning, when they went to bed their thoughts and minds continued to buzz in consideration and it was fully ten minutes before enquiries for my comfort ceased to be fired through the doorway. It was wonderful in their otherwise unvaried lives, it was an honour, it was almost their idea of heaven to have a stranger to sleep under the thatch of the house that Arthur had built with his very hands and to be entertaining the only Englishman they knew, their only compatriot apart from two or three missionaries now long since departed, was something that filled their patriotic hearts with pride. I slept like a log after the adventures of the day, but Arthur and Martha talked long into the early hours of the morning and to use Martha's words 'it was most almost daylight' before she eventually got to sleep shortly to be woken to make Arthur's breakfast, for off-loading was to start as soon after daybreak as possible.

I too was up early. After the comforts of a night in a proper bed and a roof over my head, I decided to go down to the military encampment to see how Jack and the soldiers had fared with the elements.

Seventeen of them had spent the night ashore, and they had been fairly comfortable, albeit a little cramped. I thanked my lucky stars that I had a proper home into which I could retire. I cannot conceive the misery I would have gone through had I been forced to share these tents of six or seven a piece and although I always came down for meals, including breakfast, the thought that I might be required to live there with the mob forever haunted me during the first days. Jack, as an officer, shared a comparatively spacious tent with Captain Roberts and, if I remember rightly, Sergeant Major Bowles (Great War ribbons up and in charge of the Sappers) and his quartermaster Sergeant Major Copping were also in a similarly comfortable position. But I, as a mere Flight Sergeant, would have been a miserable companion in a tent of six others.

During the course of the morning when off-loading was well under way, Captain Roberts, Jack, Sgt. Bowles and I deemed it diplomatic to pay a call on Mrs. Repetto, the head island women. When we reported at her house, her dignified face lit up with a smile of satisfaction that we should recognise her authority, but as an old friend only I could notice it. We were ushered into her best room, boarded out with wood from ships which have been wrecked on the island years ago, and close to the ceiling we noticed the nameplate of one of these, *Mabel Clark,* in large letters.

Stores being landed from the *Dunnottar Castle*.

Tea was soon brought in for she asked to be excused to put the kettle on. The conversation was rather one sided for the Tristanites were very shy of strangers and for three or four to enter the house at once was asking a bit much of the old lady, who has never been in the 'outside world'.

I naturally did most of the talking, and I was very keen that the others should get a good impression of the islanders and did not lead her off into topics of conversation which she would not understand.

The 6 April was not a terribly good day for maritime operations and the soldiers on board, in the boats and on the beaches were having their work cut out. Most of the island men were helping but, as the military personnel were under orders to carry out the work themselves and not to delegate work in any way to the islanders, there was a slight feeling of estrangement between the two parties. The islanders could not make out whether or not they were expected to help. It was their custom to help on such occasions and offered without any thought whatsoever of remuneration. They helped to get things ashore on the arrival of ships as a matter of course; in any case if one wanted to be mercenary, the chances were much in their favour that they stood to gain much in rendering assistance.

At the same time, and from the other side, there was a feeling that these quiet and mysterious islanders, who were so shy, good-mannered and well-speaking, could not be of much assistance for we had not only the advantages of education and a thorough knowledge of the various branches of engineering we represented, but we also had proper equipment, with wooden boats in place of their canvas, steel ropes and block and tackle in place of their scrappy lengths of frayed lanyard and each one confident in his ability to get the job in hand completed in the shortest length of time, seeing that we had had practice in beach operations in Simon's Bay, in the Cape.

After two or three days, therefore, the islanders gradually thought they had better drop out and leave the job to those sent down to the island especially for the purpose. Jack and I being members of the Air Force had our own interests and erected temporary screens and rain gauges, for we had already started to keep regular meteorological observations.

We put up the first instruments not far from Jack's tent on Little Beach Point. The barometer was housed in the old almost derelict mission house, built on the site where I had stayed four years previously as a member of the Norwegian Scientific Expedition.

In this historic building where Revd Wilde had lived after our departure, isolated about half a mile from the rest of his flock at the Settlement, 'Tubby' Brinkworth, our only naval rating, had quartered himself in one of the hospital beds and in another corner he had started to install his wireless equipment. As soon as possible he was to arrange communication with the Cape and our weather reports in code were to be transmitted daily. But things were not too easy for him in so confined a space and, although he managed to rig up his petrol motor and generator outside in a potato hut or outhouse of sorts, much that he wanted was still on board and many things went wrong. Eventually, by 20 April, weather reports for the first time in the history of the island were being transmitted to the Cape and Tubby had won his battle.

Three days after our arrival the weather took a very bad turn for the worse and the ship had to lie a mile or so away from land to prevent being driven ashore. Joe Repetto created a great impression in the eyes of the soldiers by swimming out naked through the heavy surf to attach a rope to a buoy they had anchored a few yards off the beach, but it was quite clear nothing useful could be accomplished. We had come at the wrong time of the year, for in the winter months storms in these latitudes can reach amazing violence! We were to experience much worse before our time was out.

The men, therefore, were ordered to build a road, for there was nothing more than a bullock cart track up from Big Beach to the plateau above. On board we had with us a proper petrol tractor and it would never be able to negotiate Big Beach Road in its present condition.

Jack at this stage showed very great consideration and kindness to me and volunteered to do most of the few meteorological duties we had to do. As an old friend I was aching at every moment to get amongst the islanders in their homes, for we had much to talk about together. I also had my movie camera with me and desired to take as much of the islanders as I could before they were spoilt by civilisation. That was my idea at the time, I never used a single foot of film, unfortunately, on our own operations on the beach. Film was scarce and I considered that I needed every foot for the islanders, for they had never been filmed properly before. In fact, no complete feature film has ever been made of these people and mine was to be the first to record their way of living. During my first few weeks I was able to catch them in colour film spinning, carding wool, sailing their boats, and engaged in many other activities. Jack found great amusement and instruction in accompanying me at times on my expeditions. Both of us had still cameras, and many opportunities arose to use them to the best advantage. Jack was a bit of an artist, and even in those early days I prevailed upon him to make me some sketches which I said I intended to include in a book I hoped to write some day. He let me have some of his sketches in which he captured a remarkable likeness of the people.

A tricky relationship had to be solved soon after our arrival. Because of their inherent courtesy towards visitors, the islanders addressed every soldier as 'sir', whereas only the two captains and possibly the sergeant-major were actually entitled to such respect! The islanders were tactfully requested to desist.

During our excursions in the Settlement, wherever we went, Jack and I had tea and sometimes doughy buns, locally known as 'cake', showered upon us and to refuse their hospitality was quite out of the question. It was a hard task to eat these stodgy buns without butter and some were made from rank flour! But that was not the islanders' fault. They had saved it months for special occasions like Whitsuntide, and gave us their last. The tea, too, was musty, but we soon got used to it and as they became more and more friendly with us, so we were able eventually after several days to take matters into our own hands and refuse it without causing offence. Besides, although we were meteorologists, we did have some work to do and had to leave to hand in weather reports for the wireless.

Every islander wanted to talk with me about the Norwegians whom they had loved so much in the past. With the European war in full swing they were worried for their safety. I was of little use in consoling them for I had the sad news to impart that I last heard from Dr Christophersen in 1940 in which year Germany invaded that lovely country. He and the others might well, we thought, have died fighting for their country and it did not pay to discuss such things with people so sensitive as these, for Martha would break into tears at the slightest opportunity. With so little interest other than their own and so little experience of the callousness of man, these people were very sensitive and their emotions were easily kindled in that manner.

Jack and I although having a comparatively easy time compared with the soldiers on the beach were nevertheless playing our role in other directions. We were diplomats, and were doing all we could to foster good feeling between the islanders and the 'invaders'. We explained to them the necessities for such actions in wartime and where misunderstandings had occurred we did our best to smooth matters out.

As day succeeded day, and not much headway had been made landing stores, it gradually dawned on the 'powers that be' that perhaps after all there was some hidden reserve of energy and a useful supply of manpower in the male island population. It was decided that if any headway was to be made at all, the islanders would have to be drawn in to help lock, stock and barrel to make use of their knowledge of the seas, their boats and their muscles, for they had already proved to the muscular soldiers that, man for man, the Tristanites could carry much heavier loads than they.

On the morning of 8 April, therefore, Roberts asked me to go and see if Willie the Chief could lend us a man to help on the beach. At seven o'clock that morning the soldiers on the beach were amazed to see three times their own number of men coming down to help. In the place of the one man I had asked for, Willie sent down the whole island and we soon took advantage of their services. Jack and I joined in too and parties were organised to execute various difficult tasks. Logs, boarding and scaffolding were thrown over the sides of the ship in the hope that they would be driven ashore either by the wind or the tide. They went careering off towards a district known as Tommy's Eyeloose and had to be rescued. The 'sea-worthy' raft, *Hopeful*, had not been able to live up to her name and was driven ashore and already lay half-buried in the sand. A second was washed against the rocks and smashed up like matchwood, for very little will stand up to the Tristan seas. Buoys anchored in the bay were also driven ashore and the position really looked hopeless. And who could have blamed them, the soldiers soon reverted to the most disgusting language, although often enough common talk in the 'outside world', and the islanders looked on open-mouthed and amazed, for they did not understand some of the awful words used. I had told them not to take any notice of what they said, but things got to a pitch when Johnnie said 'but you can't help but take notice'.

However, much work was now being done and with the added labour and boating capacity the rate of landing went up double.

Drums of petrol, cases of food, wood for building temporary encampments and tools were but some of the equipment that were needed by this preliminary survey party. It all took time when such thing as quays, jetties, wharves and piers were unknown. To have built even a temporary one we soon were to learn would have been a waste of time, for the swells which occasionally 'hit' Big Beach were so powerful that they could carry all before them and there were no other suitable places. Tristan is exposed on every shore and the elements appear to delight in running amok in these latitudes.

The morning of the 9th was appalling, so bad that the ship decided to go off on a cruise. When she did not appear for several hours we began to doubt whether her intentions were honourable, perhaps she had been sent a message which we had not received and gone to the Cape. Egged on with a feeling of frustration, the gallant sappers reverted once more to road building, and even put in drums to carry off flood water at culverts but it was all of a temporary nature and not designed to last longer than was necessary.

Jack, who was to leave the island in a few months when all was complete when the meteorological station was ready and in working condition, decided that he would like to see something of the island while he had the chance. One day we called upon Sidney Glass as a guide and climbed the 1,000ft cliffs at Burntwood several miles away on to the 'top of the base' as the islanders call the lower slopes of the mountain. This was the land of long grass and tree-ferns, but they grazed no cattle here. It was problematical to get them up there and the upper slopes of the mountain were almost perpetually enshrouded in cloud like the 'tablecloth' on Table Mountain in the Cape.

We did not have much time at our disposal on that occasion and went no further than The Knobs, 3,000ft above sea level. Here I examined my old camping site of four years ago and it was interesting to see how the whole place had become overgrown with what the islanders call sower grass. This is actually not a grass at all, but a weed which is edible and has a sour tasting leaf rather like wood sorrel. It appears that, after clearing a site of its tree ferns, this sower grass had just been waiting for the opportunity to spread, for the soil up here is very fertile and the

Captain Sayers, South African Engineering Corps, sketched by Capt J B Hattle rainfall must be at least one hundred inches in a couple of months.

We took a donkey from the Bluff back to the Settlement and slept like logs that night, but for Jack it had been just sufficient to whet his appetite for greater things to come on the following day.

The night of 11-12 April is a night which I never forgot and one of the most unpleasant I have spent in the whole of my life.

Jack decided that he would like to climb the peak and I was willing to accompany him to see if anything remained of my survey beacons of four years ago, for I had four times been to the very top already. The climb from sea level to top, which is 6,760ft above sea-level, occupies not only the greater part of the day but also a great deal of energy and one is inclined to become tired and retire before halfway up if not used to such strenuous exercise. The ascent to the top is not impossible, but it is not easy. There were what the islanders called 'some h'ugly spots' on the side of the 2,500ft cliffs at the back of the Settlement, although the rest of the way was nothing more than a tough climb.

I had heard that there was quite a large cave at 2,000ft close to the edge of the base and I suggested that it might be a good place for us to spend the night. If we went up as far as that today, I said, we should not have so far to go on the morrow; but Arthur Rogers and John the Baptist Lavarello both of whom I called as guides, warned us that the cave had a reputation for being damp and was a bit 'leaky'.

Rather than walk to the Peak in a day I was almost prepared to withstand anything, but at this stage I did not know that for which I had bargained. Jack, Arthur, John the Baptist and I packed some food and blankets in our rucksacks and set off for the cave an hour or two before sunset. After a hard climb we arrived at the cave just as it was getting dark. Once inside it was impossible to leave, for it is situated in the centre of the cliff face which is almost perpendicular and had to be reached by hanging on with both legs, both hands and your teeth at the same time (almost), otherwise you fall 1,000ft below.

Seeing that it had started to rain outside the possibilities of it clearing for an ascent to the Peak looked very remote. I thought that even a leaky, drippy or a flooded cave would be better than anything else and once inside we felt moderately secure and warm. We carried up a lot of wood, and all huddled round a camp fire

Captain Roberts, South African EngineeringCorps, sketched by Capt J B Hattle on which we boiled tea and cocoa as we felt we desired it.

Drip, drip, drip from the roof down the back of our necks was not so bad as long as the fire was alight and we sat cracking jokes, but when I turned in there wasn't a single level space to lie down on in the whole cave. By lying in a slanting position against a fairly smooth rock, the drip, drip, drip on my oilskin gradually started to torment and rest was impossible! I tossed and I turned. I moved from this rock to that, yet it was impossible to get away from the water. Jack close at hand had an officer's flea-bag, and the water did not make such a noise on his canvas. Johnnie and Arthur, on the other hand, were not so worried but then they were not comfortable for they had no room in which to lie in this tiny cave and we were trying to get to sleep sitting bolt up-right with the water dripping on their capes!

Several times I gave the matter up and woke the others from their state of semi-slumber which they seemed to have managed to enter better than me. A match was set to the fire again and more cocoa boiled. Again I tried to sleep and I asked if we couldn't go home. That, I was quite rightly informed, was out of the question. It was as dark as pitch and the mouth of the cave opened onto a 1,000ft drop. I have never known time to move so slowly. Each minute seemed the length of an hour. About four o'clock in the morning, after not having slept a wink, Arthur said I managed to doze off, but by five o'clock I was requesting

a cup of tea and a peep outside told us that we were enveloped in several thousand feet of cloud. It was hours before it got light again but it was not long before we had opened a tin of bully, washed down with hot tea. There was little else to do apart from drink.

When we were ready with our rucksacks slung once more on our backs, we debated the wisdom of proceeding on our venture in a thick Scots mist and driving rain, but seeing that we were only a couple of hundred feet from the edge of the base, we decided to scale this last short distance in the event of the weather clearing. More scrambling brought us there within twenty minutes and we found the old Norwegian rain gauge amongst the tree ferns, left there to measure the rainfall from our previous visit. It was full, of course, as it hadn't been emptied for years and in the misery of the driving dampness of the cloud which surrounded us as we tried to light a fire to boil more drink! I wondered how many times the gauge had overflowed its brim during the last four years.

Surgeon Lt. Cdr. E J S Woolley R.N.V.R. officer commanding H.M.S. Job 9, sketched by Capt J B Hattle

It was quite useless to proceed. The will was there and we could see that the islanders thought we were mad, for if we once got lost thousands of feet above the heads of our companions below, who were safe and sound in quite another world, we may lose our heads and some may never return.

It did not take us long to return to the Settlement for it was a sheer drop of 2,500ft all the way down. In places, we sat on our backsides and just slid down the face of the cliffs, for we were practically soaked through to the skin and the long wet grass made a lovely toboggan run!

When we emerged through the base of the clouds at 1,000ft I uttered a sigh of relief as the houses below came into view. The friendly sound of the ship's anchor chains with a procession of small boats working, between the shore looked to all the world like a group of slow moving water beetles. It told us that men and islanders were busy getting the last stores ashore.

"Thank God, Arthur. I thought you was all lost up on the hill. It ain't fit for nothing up there in this weather. I'se very glad to see you all back", said Martha as she greeted us with a hot pot of tea waiting on the hearth.

She had kept a look out as they always do and as soon as she had seen us emerge through the clouds had stoked the fire and prepared the tea.

Arthur lost no time in giving Martha the story of the restless night we had spent in the cave, and for the next eighteen months, as the story became generally known. I was often reminded of this night of hell but it was all in good fun, for having at last attained fairly moderately level ground again, I could relax. I slept for hours that day and vowed I would never again spend a night with an oilskin over me in a drip, drip, drippy cave. It sounded like pebbles hitting a hollow drum.

On 15 April, ten days after the arrival of the ship, news came ashore that everything was on dry land and Captain Bunbury was not only ready but only too anxious to return to the Cape. He had most dutifully carried out the instructions given him and we had been lucky in that we had not been troubled by the enemy. Before him lay another adventurous trip alone across nearly 1,000 miles of open South Atlantic, and the longer this was delayed, so the more he had cause to worry.

Something, however, had to be done to repay in some manner the Tristan islanders for the splendid work they had put in. Without their assistance the ship would have had to remain another week, and what was more, their services had been free. There was little that could be done. Spare wood, such as packing cases, were thrown overboard, and they were given the opportunity to trade with the ship's company. But Captain Bunbury thought hard and he realised that in the ship's cinema he had something which they would not only appreciate but had never in their lives seen before! He therefore invited all the men and women on the island over the age of fourteen to be his guests for morning tea, a cinema show and lunch.

The islanders were very thrilled at the prospects but some concern was caused when the women, especially the older women, contemplated the dangerous task of climbing aboard on a rope ladder up the twenty to thirty feet of perpendicular side of the ship! Eventually we had a signal sent aboard explaining the trouble and requesting that if possible the companion ways be lowered. By nine o'clock Captain Bunbury stood at the head of the steps shaking hands with the one hundred and twenty five persons who had accepted his kind invitation. It was a wonderful day and the sea was as calm as a mirror. If only it had remained like that on the day of our arrival, the off-loading would have been completed in two days instead of ten. It is amazing what the weather can do in these latitudes.

'C' Deck on the starboard side had been laid out with tables and benches and was thickly decorated with flags and bunting. As the women stood aside in shy groups after greeting the Captain, they were asked to take places for tea, the sailors doing their best to make them feel at home. But this was hardly possible for some had never ever been aboard a ship before; those who had, had been equally shy some years ago when luxury liners on world or South Atlantic cruises visited the island and likewise invited the local population aboard. Few words, therefore, very few indeed, with the exception of 'Yes, Sar' and 'No, Sar' emanated from these one hundred and twenty five souls who were amazingly good-mannered and well behaved.

Tea over, they were organised into approximately a dozen groups of ten in each and taken all over the ship by sailors and officers sightseeing. Things they had never in their lives seen before, such as big guns, telephones, loudspeakers, and electric light, the men had seen electricity before on passing ships, of course, were all demonstrated and they thought the cabins were wonderful little houses. Eventually as they thawed out a little, and it was never more than a little, as sailors' antics here and there caused laughter and some even succeeded in getting one or two of the island girls to say 'hello' down the ship's microphone. Needless to say such things caused peals of laughter, especially when unintentional remarks such as 'What I say?', 'Where?' and 'Will it bite?' were just as plainly audible throughout the ship.

I did my best rushing around helping Islanders who had either got detached from their parties or who were standing about in dazed bewilderment. By midday, when they had seen practically all there was to see they all filed along to 'C' deck once more where a proper meal awaited them.

Once more silence was golden as many partook of the best and most varied meal they had ever had in their lives, for besides soup, steak and kidney pie, with ample rolls and butter, they had sweets in the nature of tinned pineapple and custard. This latter, rare commodity was one of the most favoured of foodstuffs to these people who very seldom see it.

There were one or two rather trying scenes during lunch. One sailor doing his best to be friendly by sitting next to one of the island women caused her so much embarrassment attempting to press food on her, which she did not obviously want, she broke into tears! My blood boiled, but there was little I could do for I hate to offend and it was thought in any case that he was slightly the better for liquor. This was but the start of difficult times to come, for the mental peace of mind of the islanders was my chief concern throughout the subsequent months that followed.

Naval galley and messing quarters of *HMS Job 9*

We had expected the islanders to eat a tremendous lot, but this was far from the mark. Second helpings were more refused than accepted and we wondered whether they were too shy to eat more. When, however, it was obvious that nothing more would be eaten, sailors cleared away and the ship's mouth organ and guitar band entertained them with a few tunes as a prelude to their next excitement, the first cinema show of their lives.

At half past two Captain Bunbury collected his guests once more in the clearance on 'C' deck and addressed them. Those that saw him will never forget his manner of delivery, for he had adopted a special technique. The gist of the speech was one of thanks for all that the islanders had done in getting the cargo ashore, together with his best wishes to them in their future, no matter what it had in store. The technique he adopted, however, caused such an otherwise short message to be delivered in a full twenty minutes, for in order to drive home all he said, everything was repeated in various ways at least twice, and he accompanied his delivery with multifarious expressions of the face and waving of the hands! I had asked him, as a matter of fact, previously to speak distinctly, to use simple words and to repeat anything he wanted to drive home in particular a couple of times. He almost overdid the good work, but the islanders thoroughly enjoyed his speech and thought he was one of the nicest captains that had ever come to the island.

Trading was done between the island men and sailors, bartering, and just after three o'clock in the afternoon everyone was ordered ashore. I was preceded down the companionway by Willie Repetto, the Chief, who was one of the last to leave. As we stepped into the boat waiting alongside we heard the anchor chains straining up the side of the bows. By four o'clock on this, the 15th day of April 1942, we pulled away from her sides with islanders from the boat and sailors from the ship giving 'three cheers' in turn.

She flew bunting which we were told meant GOOD LUCK and as she pulled away to the east'ard bound for the Cape, a farewell blast on her siren told us that we were now left to fend for ourselves, isolated on an island in the centre of the great South Atlantic. Work lay ahead, and for the second time in my life I was to participate in its completion.

With the departure of the *A.M.C. Dunnottar Castle,* a big blank space appeared in the ocean as for the past ten days we had been accustomed to the sight of this large ship. No matter where you were in the Settlement, unless you bury your head in blankets, some part of the sea occupies every field of view. You cannot escape from it. The houses all faced the sea without exception and the roar of the breakers was as much a part of Tristan life as the purr of a motor car engine and the toot of a horn were to people in the outside world. The ship's departure, therefore, was a major event and her safe return was the subject of the islanders' prayers for several days to come.

Her departure, however, was also a reminder that work lay

The meteorological station, *centre,* and radio station in the distance.

ahead, and, in recognition of their labours, Captain Roberts gave his men a day's rest. But it was not long before they were engaged once more in the important programme before them. One of the first jobs was to get everything off the beach for in such exposed positions a high tide and a gale would leave nothing there the following day. The road from the beach to the Settlement was also incomplete and construction gangs were occupied here too. It was soon proved that Little Beach Point was not a suitable place for the encampment, for it was very damp and very exposed. More substantial quarters were therefore constructed near Hottentot Point at a district known as White's Garden, named after a sailor shipwrecked on Inaccessible Island 25 miles away over 100 years ago. This site was moderately close to the area which had been selected for the building of the permanent Naval establishment.

Very little meteorological equipment was ashore, the remainder of our equipment still being in the Cape with the major portion of the cargo, still to be delivered. Apart from the keeping of skeleton weather records and the dispatching of our radio reports, Jack and I were able to continue our attentions in other directions, namely, the Settlement. He became genuinely interested in the little community and the islanders grew to love him as one of the very nicest and most friendly men they had ever met. One could see that he occupied first place in their hearts, maintaining nevertheless dignity and the greatest respect.

Jack was an accomplished banjo-player and, much to the delight of the local

The naval communications station.

population, he had brought his instrument with him. We used to visit first one house then another in the evenings at the invitation of some of my closest old islander friends, for our visits were popular. He played songs for hours which the islanders lost no time in learning. *Little Sir Echo, Somebody Stole My Gal, Just an Echo* and *Don't take My Sunshine, My Only Sunshine* were some of his, and their, favourites and they listened in intense admiration until at times the less shy joined in. Perhaps fifty years ago, a shipwrecked sailor awaiting the call of a ship to take him back to civilisation possibly did the same thing, in which case the present grandparents had witnessed such concerts before. But as for the greater part of the island folk, it was something quite new and wonderful.

Another of our pastimes was taking walks in the vicinity of the Settlement but after the cave incident I discouraged the more ambitious schemes. We were often accompanied by some of the island boys who were too young to work on the beach and were not otherwise occupied on account of the absence of a school. Here again Jack's other qualifications came to the fore and he amused them for hours conjuring. But Dennis and Harold Green and Lindsay Repetto, three very nice fellows, were wide awake and not to be fooled. 'Its up your sleeve!' and 'No you ain't done eat it, it's in your pocket'. This showed that the level of intelligence of many of the island children was on a par with any in the world and the fact that there were no educational facilities on the island gave us cause for regret.

I meanwhile continued to operate my movie camera, but there was something far more important to be done, and I probably was the only person to handle the matter. The previous Anglican missionary who had been on the island during the Norwegian Expedition days of 1937-1938 had made himself unpopular with the islanders in various ways, one of which was by censoring all the inhabitants' private postal mail destined for the outside world.

The Norwegians and I believed this to be an infringement of their basic liberties, though as visitors to the island we had no cause to interfere. However, there were other reasons why the British Government wished to remove the gentleman from the island, but it was not an easy task for them given the problems of operating shipping in dangerous waters in war time.

The delay had caused some islanders to abandon the church which had served the island for over one hundred years and rumour had it that this would cause a split in the unity of the devout community. I was called upon to reason with the defectors and to inform that within the next few weeks, when the full naval staff would arrive with the remaining stores, there would not only be a full-time naval Surgeon Commander to supervise the whole island but a full-time naval chaplain who would be responsible for both naval and civilian spiritual affairs.

With full agreement from the chief islander, I was authorised to carry out this provisional task of reassurance, with the result that within the next few weeks, twenty to thirty defectors had returned to the church. When the Revd C P Lawrence arrived from *H.M.S. Cilicia* on the 10 May 1942, he found his full congregation awaiting him and a workforce ready to help in landing another 1000 tons of stores before this ship could leave the island.

The most important passenger on *H.M.S. Cilicia* was Surgeon Lieutenant-Commander E J S Woolley, R.N.V.R., the naval doctor destined to be in command of the shore-based naval establishment for the next two years. He was also to be responsible for the civilian population during his residence. He was accompanied by his wife, Vivian, their small family and extra naval ratings.

H J Heighway takes a reading and launches a weather balloon.

Revd C P Lawrence R.N.V.R., Naval Padre.

South African engineers.

Sgt. Major Bowles and Islanders.

Exploring the Settlement

During our stay on the island it was interesting to observe and to record the islanders' various activities and their ability to craft most of what they needed from local resources or that which had been swept up onto the beaches.

The islanders used their one and only island bush (*Phylica arborea*) as fuel in their homes both for cooking and heating. The fuel was either procured by chopping it down on the mountain side, allowing it to dry and then carting it on the backs of donkeys to the Settlement or by sailing round the beaches in their boats in search of driftwood. Arthur Rogers, Johnnie Green and Joe Repetto would be up, well before sunrise, setting off from the stony and kelp-strewn Little Beach, situated about half a mile from the Settlement, to sail round Big Point in their canvas dinghy in search of driftwood which was plentiful after some of the gales and storms which swept the island in the wintertime. Heavy inundations of sometimes two or three inches of rain in the night caused avalanches of soil and water to slide down the mountainside into the sea taking with them thousands of bushes which were eventually washed up onto the various beaches around the island to be collected when the opportunity arose.

At Little Beach, Arthur, Johnnie and Joe hauled their dinghy up onto the beach, laden up to the gunwales with their first load of wood for the day. The boat was heavy and had to be pulled to safety above the wash of the waves. The men stood alongside the boat and threw the wood onto the beach, piece by piece, while their wives and some boys stacked it into bundles. On such occasions as these, when the men sometimes came home wringing wet through to the skin, a cup of tea was the most welcome reward for their labours. The women always thought all day of their men folk when they were away and eagerly watched the horizon below Big Point for the first signs of the boats rounding the Bluff.

Johnnie's wife, Sophia, walked down the steep little Beach Road, tea-pot in hand, and a stampede started down to the beach toward the tea.

"Sar, would you care for a cup of drink?" proffered Sophia as she advanced

Islanders hauling a dinghy loaded with driftwood on Little Beach.

towards us with cup and teapot in hand after a consultation with herself to make sure that she was doing the right thing and would not cause us offence.

"It is very kind of you Sophia, but hadn't you better keep your tea for the men? They'll want it badly, and they're a bit wet too."

"That's alright Sar, I guess they won't drink half what I got for them in this pot. T'is a big pot, Sar, an' it hold enough for eight men," she insisted.

She gave us each a cup while the men dried their feet and put on their footwear.

We finished our tea and shook out the dregs onto the beach. The men had their tea while Sophia, Martha and May started to sort out the wood into three piles, one for each of the three families who had been engaged on the work. As we left the beach, three boys, Harold Green, Barnet Repetto and Lindsay Repetto, drove donkeys onto the beach to cart up the wood; Lindsay helping Arthur and Martha who had no children of their own. The donkeys had been introduced to Tristan some one hundred years before from St. Helena.

The men sorting out their wood on the beach did not work in silence for their sense of humour was far too acute to remain dormant for long.

"What time did you get up this morning Jim?" I asked Arthur, for 'Jim' is his nickname, although I did not know how he acquired it originally.

Women welcome the men with mugs of tea after a day's work at sea.

"Old Jim no lie-a-bed," he replied with a good natured grin stretching from ear to ear. "When there's work to be done, me an' Johnnie an' Joe believes in getting it done. We ain't like them what sit an' smoke all day at their gable ends while other people walk out the patches to work, I guess we was on the beach long before you was down there on your mets. (6 a.m. weather reports)."

This was not boasting and we decided that, as they were keen on getting off for another trip so that they could get home by midday, we would leave them and stroll towards the Settlement. To keep one's household supplied with wood it was necessary to make such trips once or twice a month throughout the year, but if there had been no recent floods they had to climb several thousand feet up the cliffs and collect wood in a much more dangerous and laborious manner. Some islanders had slipped and been killed collecting firewood on the mountainside. As we ascended the steep incline which leads from Little Beach to the grassy slopes of the Settlement above the three boys passed us with donkeys on their way back down to bring up more wood.

On calm days, such as this, there was always great activity in the neighbourhood of the beaches for the islanders have learnt to take any opportunities as they offer themselves as the wintertime swells could be so rough and of such duration that it was impossible to launch a boat for ten days or a fortnight at a time.

We were not surprised, as we reached Boat harbour in Little Beach Road, to see Hubert Green and Andrew Glass with their dinghy oars over their shoulders walking to the beach to get their boat ready for a bit of fishing.

"Good morning, Sar," they said as they raised their caps.

"What are you doing?" we enquired.

"We's going off fishing Sar," they replied.

Over on the left about one hundred yards from where we were walking close to Little Beach Point was the old Norwegian Scientific Expedition House in which Dr Erling Christophersen's men and I lived during their four month sojourn on the island in 1937-38. Since we left in 1938 it was taken over by Reverend Harold Wilde as his mission headquarters, but being in such an exposed position and after his departure it soon fell into disrepair and has now almost completely been broken down, the stone and wood being used for building elsewhere.

On Little Beach Point itself was the island flagstaff and an old sixteen pounder cannon, left on the island in 1816 when troops were sent to occupy the island in the name of the British Crown in Napoleonic days. The remains of a small piece of the earthwork of the original fort were still visible. We heard the noise of someone using a ripping saw above the roar of the sea which had been shut out by the bank. Thomas Glass, Rudolph Rogers, one of the twins, and another were busy making repairs to their boat which had been drawn up onto the grassy plateau for the purpose.

The last time they had taken their boat out someone had dropped a heavy load of wood onto the starboard side gunnel which, being old, was smashed. In a land where such a thing as a convenient length of wood and band-saws were unknown, the ripping of pieces of driftwood into lengths suitable for repairing boats was a long and tiring task indeed.

Thomas was a good carpenter and he appreciated our visit so much that when he stopped to mop his brow and hand over the saw to his twin, he offered us one of his cigarettes which he had bartered for a pair of homespun stockings in the ship that passed some days ago. No matter if we had taken his last cigarette, from his point of view, 'What we ain't got we can do without and won't miss' he philosophically replied to our suggestion that we will run him short. Thomas is one of the nicest, most intelligent and industrious of men on the island and has never feared a spot of hard work since the day he was born.

In the distance, at the foot of Chief's flax garden, we noticed someone engaged on the construction of a new dinghy. As we proceeded up the slope towards Big

Watron, the island water supply which flows down the eastern side of the Settlement. The 'home' sheep grazing above Derrick caught our eye. This prompted us to inquire whose sheep they were and why they were called the 'home' sheep. There were some three to four hundred sheep on the Settlement plateau and all were privately owned. A couple of hundred of these usually grazed close to the houses, these were called the 'home' sheep whereas the remainder which were not so tame and usually grazed out the Molly Gulch and the Bluff were known as the 'farm' sheep.

Islanders rounding up sheep for night-time penning to produce manure for potato crops.

The industrious and 'rich' islanders possessed as many as thirty to forty sheep, the poorer ones perhaps only five or ten. But the poor were not unfortunate: the reason for their small supply was laziness, for these were the people who had possibly more sheep than others and in hard times had just killed off their stocks to eat good meat instead of doing a day's fishing or a few extra hours work in their ground. Many missionaries who visited the island were appalled at the poverty of some and succeeded, in some cases, against the better judgement of the industrious islanders, in obtaining sheep for these unfortunate ones so that they can get a 'fair' chance of building up their stocks. But the story had always, without exception, had the same result, like the idea of communism it soon broke down because after a few months they had killed the sheep they were given and were in the same boat once more. A leopard cannot change its spots. Every man had exactly the same chance on Tristan as any other and if a person could not make good he had only himself to blame.

In order that the islanders could distinguish between one another's sheep, they had an ingenious system of marking their ears with splits, cuts and 'pieces off'. Every man had his own mark and hence his own sheep. No two combinations were alike and when the lambs were born young islanders could be seen going out to the Bluff, sometimes on Sunday mornings after Church, armed with pocket knives to mark their sheep. John the Baptist Lavarello has the mark 'a split in the right and a split in the left.' Johnnie Green, 'a piece under the right and a piece off the top of the left'. Cattle were also marked in this way, but donkeys were seldom marked. That was because not every family possessed a donkey and few possessed more than two. It was therefore much easier to distinguish them and every man knew his own, not only by its size and colour, but also its manners and temper.

The island sheep have never been given names of any description but a few donkeys had been so honoured. John the Baptist has a donkey called 'Cabby' which was notorious and had the awful habit of breaking into other people's gardens and eating their flax and tussock. 'Cabby' was too old to work and there was some question of doing away with him. Gordon Glass' 'Black fire' took a lot of beating to get him out to the Patches but when he was 'pointing for home' he would gallop at a fair speed. 'Nancy', 'Tibby', and 'Bearwig' were the only other recorded names I was able to collect and I think these were names used by some of their grandfathers and were now probably extinct.

As we entered the village from across Big Watron a hammering was going on in a substantially built old house, where Gordon and Susan Glass' family lived. Gordon was busy on some carpentry job and our curiosity got the better of us. We paused and knocked on his door.

"Morning Susan, we were on our way to your mother's and wondered what Gordon was up to, so we thought we would have a look in and see".

"You's very welcome Sar, of course you can come an' see Gordon, he's putting up a new 'tition (partition) 'tween our bedroom an' the kitchin. Go through and see how he's getting on".

We walked along the tiny passage into the kitchen, where we could see Gordon and Joe Repetto, who was helping him, with jackets off and sleeves rolled up busily engaged in nailing pieces of boarding, originally pieces of old packing cases, onto up-rights.

"Good morning, Sar," Gordon and Joe greeted us in unison.

Joe told us that his greatest trouble was nails. "If only you could get nails on Tristan you would know what you was doing an' the work would come h'easier. We all have to cut up a bit of wire when we have no nails and make them ourselves."

We sat down in the kitchen, my friend on an old sea chest and me on a home made bench. Gordon related the story of how his house used to belong to old Betty Cotton who died at the grand old age of ninety some fifteen years ago. She was the last of the Cotton family and with her death, the name became defunct although there was plenty of Cotton blood on the island. Susan in the meanwhile has placed the 'pot' on the fire having sent Ada out to the hut for a piece of wood.

The kettle boiled and Susan put her last tea spoon of tea into the teapot and the beverage, beloved throughout the world, was pressed upon us. We were a little thirsty after our stroll up from the beach and as it was already getting on for ten o'clock the tea was most welcome.

"I ain't got no sugar, I'm sorry sir."

"We don't mind. The chief thing, Susan, is that it's wet"

"Sure, it's wet, Sir," Susan smiled as she appreciated the joke.

Gordon and Joe were likely to be hammering all day so we told them that we must be on our way.

As we walked out of the house a little girl, poor, but not too badly dressed, was not embarrassed by our presence on account of our sudden exit.

"Aunt Susan, Mamma says please could you let her have a plate of 'pigs taters', she say daddy's going off fishing an' will send you down a bit of fish when he get in." she asked.

"Why you all can't grow your taters same as everyone else on the island, I don't know," says Susan who knows well that 'pigs taters' were not for the pigs but to feed the lazy family. With an 'excuse me, sir' as we departed, we glanced back and see her going into the hut with a tin to give the child the desired commodity.

After rain, the 'road' in the vicinity of Susan's was a bit soggy and as we crossed a small stream we noticed Alice Glass placing some washing on her wall.

"Sidney is gone out aft to grass (after grass) and expects he will be back before 12 o'clock for his dinner. He ain't gone so far, he gone back of Marigens where you got your two patches, Mr Crawford, an' he got Lewis (his brother-in-law) an' a couple of donkeys so he won't be long", she informed us, followed by,

"Trina, what you doing now? I reckon if I catch you playing with my flat iron again I'll give you a hammering as you'll never forget," she shouted as Trina screamed from inside the house. Alice was gone like a flash.

A little bit further on, Doris Lavarello was milking her cow. Doris was a quiet girl and had not much to say for herself as we passed by.

There were a few things of interest in connection with the island cattle. Naturally enough any cow which resented being milked had it's hind legs tied together with a bit of rope. The young boys were usually sent out along the Plateau in the morning to bring home the milk cows, which had had their calves blocked away from them on the other side of Knockfolly Gulch as soon as they were able to look after themselves. Many island cattle were giving poor milk but fresh blood, introduced in the nature of an Ayrshire bull in 1937, resulted in the improved herds. The bull was called 'Carlisle' because that was the name of the Naval ship in which he travelled from the Cape of Good Hope.

Early morning milking in the village.

Sometimes cows drank their own milk and I never knew about this until I passed a cow on the island one day with a curious piece of board tied to its nose with a nail protruding from the centre. Whenever she tried that game she gave herself a jab with the nail and decided it was not altogether a paying proposition.

A few of the cows on the island had names, but not all. These were all handed down from the 'old hands' of fifty to a hundred years ago with some that were interesting and well worth recording:

Fancy,	White leg,	Lilly,	Martin,	Nora,
Pink,	Hardy,	Hannah,	Polly,	Kiddy,
Emma,	English,	Old Podge,	Five o'clock,	Big Tit,
Long Legs,	Broken Horn,	Blackberry,	Strawberry	

Those who had a good cow in milk usually have a stream of children calling throughout the day with their jugs, tins and cups. It was not long before I got used to a knock on the door at Arthur and Martha Roger's house with the inevitable little child's 'Arnie (Auntie) Mamma ask you, please could you let her have a drop of milk'. I never heard an islander refuse anyone, except when they did not possess the desired container, and in the two years I must have heard some hundreds of requests.

Islanders and Navy personnel after church. Old Sam Swain is standing at the front left.

Boat Building

The sight of somebody building a boat up on the grass amongst the houses which we observed earlier in the morning drew us like a magnet and as we arrived at the bottom of Chief's flax garden we recognised Fred Swain as being the industrious man. Why he was working alone we forgot to ask, for when making boats the islanders usually worked together, each member of the boat's crew doing a fair part.

Boats on Tristan were never owned individually but three or four islanders clubbed together and decided to go part shares in a long boat or dinghy, whichever they desired. The dinghy, about twenty feet long was used mostly for fishing and collecting wood, whereas a long boat, twenty five to thirty feet long, was used for sailing across to Nightingale and Inaccessible Islands, twenty-five miles away when half a dozen men and large loads had to be carried. Long boats were also used for taking the men, women and children round to Sandy Point two or three times a year when the apples were ripe, returning after each day's gathering, loaded right up with tins, boxes, sacks and drums full of this their only fruit produce.

Fred doffed his cap as we approached him and showed us the various parts of his boat. I made sketches and marked down the names. The keel was made of a solid piece of the best quality hard driftwood. A false keel was nailed to the bottom to save the keel proper from wearing. The head was likewise made of good wood and, because of its curved shape, was usually made out of two pieces bolted together in the centre.

A long flat strip of steel or iron which was secured by screws or nails the whole length of the head carried along the keel a foot or two for protection as most of the island beaches were stony and the bottom part of the boats would have soon worn away by continual friction, if it were not for the irons.

"What is that hole right through the keel and iron about 18 inches forward of the stern post," I asked Fred, for it appeared to me to weaken the boat.

"This," Fred informed me, "is the plug hole. Island boats, because they are made of canvas, all leak sometimes and that's where you let the water out when you haul up on the beach".

The frame of a twenty foot dinghy under construction.

Nailed to the top of the keel on port and starboard sides, and at intervals of approximately nine inches to a foot, were the timbers of the boat which were made out of willow, if possible, otherwise apple bough or Island tree. To form the curve of the boat these were soaked in boiling water, just prior to fixing, and tied down with string to the strengthening boards. Building proceeded by propping the keel, stem and stern posts on the grass with temporary backstays. Strengthening boards, three or four in number, were made out of good quality planed wood, on port and starboard sides which were set in to the head and stern to which they were nailed and bent to the form of the boat.

When all of this had been completed the boat was a curious sight with the various lengths of timbers sticking up into the air but sawing them off to the right length was not done until the gunwales had been prepared and screwed, if they had any, to the outside of the head and stern. Copper nails were of course in great demand for boat building but were not always obtainable. However, once the gunwales were fixed into position and the timbers secured to them the latter were sawn off and the framework began to look more like a boat. As the work proceeded the pieces and stays for keeping the framework in position were temporarily secured here and there across the boat to keep it rigid and shipshape.

An islander puts the final coat of paint on the hull of a dinghy.

The next item on the programme were the slabs which usually consisted of smooth pieces of lathing, some half an inch in thickness and one and a half inches wide, which were nailed flat on the outside of the timbers in strips from stem to stern which would eventually take the canvas. To ensure that the gunwales were rigidly attached to the head, a piece of V-shaped apple wood known as bow knee was eagerly sought by the boat builders at Sandy Point, for this was one of the most important and hard to obtain brackets required for the making of their boats.

About a dozen more knees were required, of an obtuse angle shape, for securing the seats, or rather thwarts, to the strengthening boards. Long boats usually had five or six thwarts, dinghies had only three. These had to be strong enough to take the weight of the man pulling as hard as he could on an oar and special wood of robust selection was saved for this important purpose. Many Islanders were delayed in their boat building due to the absence of wood suitable for the thwarts but Fred, our islander companion, was fortunate in this respect. A piece of wood resembling a thwart, called the mast board, connected the first three thwarts and had a hole to steady the mast about two thirds the way along from the head end.

Resembling small seats in the very bow of the boat were two strips of wood arranged crosswise supported on the strengthening boards known as the head sheets; the stern sheets occupied a corresponding position in the back of the boat. Above this was the name board on which was painted the name of the boat, for most islanders liked to give names for distinguishing purposes. A curious piece of wood protruded about four inches on the port side, just forward of the stern post, which was known as the steering gear. A hole in the centre took a small loop of rope to secure an oar, used for the purpose of landing in heavy swells. The leverage obtained from an oar for steering purposes was infinitely more useful and positive in action in the dangerous swells that sometimes faced them when they reached the beaches. To rely on the rudder would certainly have caused disaster and the boat would soon have been carried beam on and thrown against the stones to be smashed into matchwood. Thimbles (eyes) of steel received the spindles attached to the rudders and an ordinary tiller furnished the steering in open water.

Long boats had six oars, three to port and three to starboard, but dinghies had only three, two on the port side and one on the starboard side, with the balance of power, due to the otherwise unequal motive force, being taken up mostly in the rudder. Of course, with two men pulling on one side of the boat and only one on the other, the former naturally did not work as hard as the latter, but when there was work to be done and an objective to be reached the single oarsman on the starboard side seemed to take on superhuman strength and, with the aid of a good cox, it was seldom that a dinghy steered a crooked course.

Once the frame was complete the next thing was to nail on thick canvas of good quality, possibly old ship and lifeboat sails, which was cut to the right length to suit the boat and nailed to the top of the length of the keel. Here a long piece of lathing known as a strip was nailed over to give a finish and, if possible, a long piece of narrow copper plate did the same work up and down the stem and stern posts. Where the canvas did not reach the gunwales, other pieces were sewn on until it was long enough. Islanders had always to be careful to nail the canvas on a fine day when it was dry, for the slightest moisture in the cloth when put on caused it to slacken in fine weather and become baggy. Just as strips secured the canvas to the keel, a wide neat board called the covering board, did the same work against the gunwales. A wash board, from bow to stern on both sides of the boat, put the finishing touch to what otherwise might have appeared as a slovenly appearance.

All that remained were the home-made rowlock gears and rowlocks, the latter of which, together with the oars, they liked to acquire ready-made from passing ships, in exchange for geese and island sheep.

The last job was the painting. Paint was one of the most vital commodities which they hoped to get from passing ships. If there was an abundance they painted the timbers and inside of the boat canvas too, because the more paint there was, the longer the wood lasted.

Then came the name which was the most important, insofar as long boats were concerned but not many dinghies possessed names. Some of the island boats were called after olden day sealers and whalers that called at the island on their way to the Antarctic in the early days of sail, but the origins of others I was not able to fathom. Here were some of the boats present on the island in 1942:

Ticket

Old Petrel

Canton (an American whaler)

Wild Rose (named after a Cape Schooner)

Phoenix (Henry Green's boat, named after a whaler)

Christophersen (named after the leader of our 1937 Norwegian Expedition)

Carlisle (called after *H.M.S. Carlisle*, 1932 and 1937)

Lorna (named by Mr Lindsay, Lay Reader)

Morning Star (originally a whaler)

British Trader (a tourist ship)

Miss England

Pincher

One dinghy had the nickname of *Darkie* but the owners did not like to admit it.

Whenever possible, and quite naturally too, the islanders always tried to take advantage of the wind and the weather sequence before setting out either around the beaches or to the other islands, for who wanted to row when a fair wind would fill your sail? The canvas from old ships' sails was cut up and sewn to form the jibs and mainsails to suit dinghies and long boats.

Having no centre boards or heavy keels, island boats would not tack against the wind, they would be blown off their course if they tried it, and so they nearly always had to rely on a following wind.

We had a long session with Fred Swain and, as the clock was approaching quarter past eleven, we decided to make a call on Mrs Repetto, Head of the Island women, for a cup of tea.

The islanders notched the underside of their plates as a means of identifying their owners.

Spinning

We approached Mrs Repetto's house by crossing over a stream, which flowed down the west side of her house and served as her water supply. We entered the small yard in front of her house and knocked on the stable-type door which was a common feature of most island houses and on fine days the top half would be swung open to admit the fresh morning air.

"Come in," piped a squeaky voice from inside the kitchen.

We hesitated in our reluctance to take possession of her hospitality too graspingly. We heard her voice again.

"Rose, go see if there ain't someone knocking on Grannie's door. I's sure I heard someone knock. Go see who it is for Grannie, there's a good girl. Grannie'll give you a bit of sugar if she's got some."

27 April 1942: Mrs Frances Repetto, Head Island Woman, pours tea on her 66th birthday for the many expected visitors.

Presently, but in a most shy manner, Rose poked her head round the corner of Mrs Repetto's kitchen-passage door and was surprised to see two strangers, although she knew me of course

"Good morning, Sar," she said shyly with her finger in her mouth beating a hasty retreat to the kitchen informing 'Granny Fan' that, "they aint h'island people what's knocking on the door."

"Come in," Mrs Repetto squeaked as she appeared on the scene, her voice piquant with age and the lines of her face portrayed character and intelligence of a high degree, bidding us enter, "Come in, I'm very pleased to see you, an' I don't know whether

Experienced carders with a bathtub of raw wool and 'rolls' ready for spinning.

you'd prefer to go in the outside room or come an' have a cup of tea with me in the kitchin? It's just as you like."

We assured her that we liked her kitchen and that we were not people for ceremony.

Mrs Repetto, being an old lady, could not work about the house as she used to in the days gone by and most of her scrubbing and dirty work was done by one of the island unmarried girls. This girl was a sort of servant and I have heard the old girl give her 'blazes' when she neglected something she should have done. The girl was of a poor family and the meals she got now and again in the Repetto household, together with the potatoes she took home, saved the girl many a day of starvation.

Grannie Fan organized tea, despatching Rose off to the Watron with the kettle for water. She blew up the fire with a pair of bellows which she said she 'had come by' years ago and presently we were sipping our tea over discussions of one thing and another. But this was a work day and we were not going to tarry long as we did not have time to hear this old island sage's views, in one direction and another, in connection with the influx of military and naval personnel.

Bridget Green with her spinning wheel showing the head, spindle and cord used to drive the wheel.

We departed and crossed once more the Watron, which ran down the west side of Mrs Repetto's house, and struck out downhill across the road past Bill and Jane Rogers' to the back of Lily's, where Mrs Repetto has told us she had 'hands' carding and spinning. Intermittent laughter coupled with the hum of the 'wheel' told us as we entered the gate that they were not only busy but happy too, though Joanie, her one and a half year old toddler, seeing us enter the yard ran screaming into the house!

Lily welcomed us with a knowing smile. We were at once struck by the similarity of her features with those of her Grandmother, Mrs. Repetto. Her sparkling eyes and intelligent appearance told us at once that here was one of the more cultured type and a girl who was capable of interesting herself in those with whom she came into contact. Although her house was untidy with the hive of industry the clean walls and mantle shelf which had escaped congestion clearly indicated cleanliness and good upbringing. Quite apart from Susan, her mother's, excellence as a mother, Lily, before she was married, was the favourite niece of my friends, Arthur and Martha Rogers, whom Fate decreed to be childless. Even when small Lily used to help them about the house and whenever Susan had too much on her hands with all the rest of the family, Lily was sent up to Martha's where she spent many a night under their protecting care.

Interested as they were in this special niece, Martha spent many hours teaching her not only to read and write but also the story of the scriptures. The trustworthiness and reliability of this girl were, in a very large part, due to her fortune in having been all but adopted in this God-loving household. This was not to praise the character of Lily in the eyes of others, but as their favourite niece I got to know her better then any of the others and was thus able to study her at closer range than any of Granny Fan's other grandchildren. Lily's eldest child, Joan, had been christened after my eldest sister in England and if she had been a boy was destined to be named after me. I therefore took a great interest in Joanie and, in my opinion, the sunshine radiated from her eyes and she was the nicest little kid I ever knew, anywhere in the world. Although her dashing screaming into the house on our approach was typical of her behaviour during the first few weeks of my visit to the island, I got to know the family so well that one day I picked her up as she screamed her head off for nothing and deposited her on the bed. From that day, until her third birthday on October 14, 1943, on which day I left the island for the Cape, Joanie and I were best friends and she followed me all round the place with our mutual affection. In her inability at two to call me by my correct name, she found a substitute in 'Uncle Coppie' and I knew that if I returned to the island she would greet me with a kiss and revert to her old nickname for me.

We entered the living-room-cum-kitchen, for being a newly married couple, Lily and Victor had a small house. We sat down on a box close to the door just clear of Emily Hagan, a girl of about sixteen or seventeen years of age who has taken possession of most of the floor space with the spinning wheel. The islanders always used an old fashioned type of hand operated wheel which must have been some centuries old and probably introduced from Scotland or England by the early settlers. We could hardly miss the wheel in the middle of the room with its intermittent hum as Emily worked it back and forwards and my friend from the 'outside world' naturally commented on the most conspicuous item.

Sitting in a row opposite us on a bench some five feet long were three elderly women, Annie Swain, Mabel Lavarello and Clara Glass. All three were busily engaged in 'carding', this being the treatment necessary to turn the wool into 'rolls' for the spinning, an art that was also a relic of olden times. Although I tried several times to put the vital twist into the rolls, which is so necessary for a good thread, I was never able to succeed to produce more than the laughs which resulted from my poor attempts.

The carders themselves resembled butter pats with in place of the grooved surface, strips of special wire carding cloth attached, which served to tease out the wool and make it into the rolls. Gangs of carders were prepared to sit the whole day at this wrist-aching task only breaking their labours for meal times and an occasional 'drop o' drink'.

It was too dark to photograph them inside so I managed to persuade them to cart everything into the open where the light was better. Just as every girl on the island when she reached her teens learned to spin, so likewise when they got older they gave way for their juniors and learned to card, this latter operation invariably being carried out by those of mature age. But the final use for the wool when completed, knitting, was the work of the female population of the island no matter whether they were ten or ninety years old! I cannot speak for the early settlers but in recent years there never existed a woman on the island who could not knit. In fact, except for Sundays when they would not pick up a single stitch, whether they were by the house or walking out to the patches to work in the ground, the women were always to be seen with needles clicking as they made pullovers, socks, stockings and comforters for their menfolk to use when they visited the other islands on cold and windy days.

When an island woman decided she wanted some carding and spinning done, and her husband has a goodly supply of wool in the hut at the back of the house, she, in this case Lily, decided with whom she liked to work. A few days before the actual day set aside, she visited these women in their homes and 'called' them to work. It was seldom that anyone ever refused, for if they refused they would have difficulty in 'calling' hands when their day came round to benefit from the work of others. However, once the day arrived they came down to the house and without much to-do got started on their work, for an efficient woman had everything ready about eight o'clock. By nine o'clock, it was breakfast time which probably consisted of a bit of cold meat and 'taters'. Dinner at one and supper at six or seven would probably be better meals and consist of roast beef or mutton and potatoes, followed in the evening by grated potato pudding with currants and a bit of sugar to give it a flavour. In a land where money did not exist the meals for the day were the only form of payment for services rendered which applied to the men too.

Alice Swain knitting, sketched by Capt J B Hattle

We observed, before we entered the house, that the women did not work in silence. True to their sex throughout the world they were never at a loss for something to say and after the introduction of Naval and Military personnel I think they became fifty times more voluble.

Shy Emily's barriers of reserve had been broken down by our good-natured exchange of information and wisecracks. The wheel stopped and she turned to Lily to ask for some fat as the wheel was a bit squeaky and the spindle was getting hot. Petrel's fat, seal oil or ordinary lubricating oil out of a drum, if they had it, was used for this purpose. Old wheels soon wore their wooden bearings to a wobble.

The construction of these 'wheels', as they called them for short, was most interesting. One day during my stay on the island I managed to get Arthur Rogers and Johnnie Repetto to make a wheel for their wives from some wood I managed to let them have. Normally they were dependent upon decent pieces of driftwood and parts of packing cases from which to manufacture their wheels and the construction of such a fast revolving piece of mechanism had to be well-balanced and the best so that the wheel itself did not wobble, which would have resulted in the band flying off.

In order that the wheel was steady the base part, with its two short and two long legs at each end, had to be made from a piece of sleeper or other hard and heavy piece of wood. The arms, one to carry the wheel and the other the spindle, were set into holes in the base and wedged fast by means of a tapered piece of wood driven into a split in each arm. The pin to hold the wheel was secured to the arm in a similar manner. A head on the top of the spindle had two holes through it parallel with the base and into these were inserted two strips of leather which formed the flexible bearing for the spindle. This bearing was one of the most remarkable parts of an island spinning wheel and why they should have adopted such a Heath Robinson arrangement was hard to fathom unless it allowed the spindle to be taken out quicker. That must have been the reason for this curious type of bearing, for to 'ball' the wool the full spindle was taken out and an empty one inserted so that the spinning continued with little loss of time. The leather bearings were held in position like much of the rest of the contraption by means of small wooden wedges which held them tight.

If the wheel was eccentric and running off-centre the band tended to fly off. To put matters right an adjustment could be made to the spindle by letting out one or other of the leather bearings to alter the eccentricity of the wheel so as not to interfere with the spinning.

The spindle was made from a piece of steel wire with a small leather flange and a home-made brass pulley firmly driven on. The end of the spindle part itself was tapered to a point to enable the thread to twist off easily in the spinning process.

One of the hardest things to make was the wheel itself and those islanders, without an eye for symmetry, sometimes produced some very odd shapes. The hub in the centre had to be made from a piece of oak and the trimming and boring of this circular piece of wood caused many a headache in a land where the lathe was unknown. Twelve pieces of strip to form the spokes had also to be planed and rounded as no wood suitable for this purpose could be grown on the island. The small ends of these were forced into small holes staggered evenly round

Asturias Rogers (aged 15), sketched by Capt J B Hattle

the hub so that they projected at equal distances away from the centre. This was done by measuring the ends with a string held at the centre and any long spokes were marked and sawn off to the correct length. Their next headache was the rim to finish the wheel. A long piece of lath or planking three inches wide and a quarter thick was prepared from anything suitable and soaked in the 'watron' for a day before it was needed to make it supple and pliable. It was then cut to an approximate length to suit the circumference of the wheel. The two ends were tapered off to form an overlap.

The centre of the rim was then marked off and nailed to one of the spokes. Carefully gripping the whole thing, it was gradually bent and nailed to each spoke in turn until it formed a continuous circle. The tapered ends then came together and, after being temporarily secured with string to take the strain, were glued, if they had any, nailed together and filed or sand-papered off smooth.

The band which ran on the outside of the rim and engaged with the pulley on the spindle was usually made from a stout piece of fishing line sewn, not tied, together at the join. A rod passed through a hole in the end of the wheel with a pin, sometimes made of wood or otherwise a piece of iron, to keep it from slipping off which made the wheel ready for use. Grease in the hub bearing assured smooth running.

Emily was having little trouble and things were going smoothly. As the three women on the bench produced the 'rolls' Emily spun the 'wosted', as they call it, taking about two hours to fill a spindle. As these were filled Lily, who was in the meantime preparing the next meal for her workers, 'balls' it off into balls about 4 inches in diameter. At the end of the day the carding was probably all finished and the women walked off home, but the following morning there was sure to be plenty more spinning as well as other work to be done. Emily returned to complete her work, or until she has "done spin" as they say. The next item on the program was the important one of twisting, for up till now the wosted is single ply.

With two balls of single thread in a basin on the floor, the end of each ball was taken and tied to the spindle of the spinning wheel. The wheel was then revolved and the double thread twisted onto the spindle. This was done until the spindle was full and then replaced by a new one. Next came another important operation, skeining. It was not desirable to ball the wosted at this stage because with the carding, spinning and twisting it had become quite dirty and would not wash in the form of a ball. Some Islanders possessed a special homemade machine, called a "skeiner", which consisted of four revolving arms on a base piece. The contraption was revolved by hand and the wool fed on from the spindles at quite a good speed. It was important to count the revolutions as the wool was measured into skeins, knots and turns. Every woman wanted to know how much wool she had 'done spin' and the quantity expressed in so-many skeins and so-and-so-many knots was the subject of conversation amongst the women for several days to come. I wondered how the scale of weights and measures used on Tristan for their measuring of wool compared with those of the 'outside world'. There were 40 turns to 1 knot and 7 knots to 1 skein.

Some 'skeiners', had a piece of springy wood which made contact with a peg in the wheel so that with each revolution a click could be heard and the wool more easily counted. After every forty turns, the wosted was knotted together by three or four pieces of wool but it was not broken. The girl skeining then carried on for another forty turns until she had two knots on her machine and these were likewise tied together but not cut. With seven knots, or one skein, she broke the thread and took the wool off her machine and started all over again. The skeins were then washed with soap and hot water and put out to dry, to be stored away and balled for when required for knitting.

The wool was never dyed as they had no dyes to use for the purpose. It was knitted up into pullovers, socks and stockings which were all white except for the 'marking', the coloured wool in this case being taken from imported woollen goods which were pulled out for the purpose. If stockings and the like did not have distinguishing marks in the way of various combinations of coloured 'markings', no one would know one pair of socks from another. Even the socks themselves could get mixed in the wash. A typical harvest from a day's spinning which Lily on this occasion was able to show was eight skeins and three knots.

That lasted her a month or two, at least, and she did not have to bother about spinning for some time. It might be, however, that to finish her last pullover she 'got the loan' of a skein from her Auntie Martha, or from someone else, and as sure as fate Martha would not delay one minute in sending her sister, Ada, up with the borrowed quantity of wool. On Tristan, as everywhere else, the sooner one paid one's debts the quicker one's state of mind was satisfied.

It was with the greatest difficulty that we refused tea at Lily's when we arrived. With our visit to Mrs. Repetto's beforehand we had ample excuse for departure, so we thought, without filling ourselves up with unnecessarily large quantities of liquid. But we tarried so long with the spinning that Lily produced, behind our backs while we were examining the construction of the wheel, two cups of the refreshing liquid which we were compelled to drink in order not to cause offence. These Islanders were all hospitality personified in this respect and would never allow a stranger to enter their house without attempting to satisfy in some way his inner man. They would use up their last drop of milk, their only remaining tea leaves and the last grain of sugar to pay their respects to a stranger who crossed their threshold. Many a time I had proof of this, the drinking of their last, but to refuse was to offend.

Women planting potatoes, near Below the Hill, two miles from the Settlement.

Housebuilding

To the west of Lily's house was the only doubled-storey house on the Island, the house of Hagan. This house, together with Susan's, Mr Repetto's and one or two others had been much better constructed than the more recent island houses, one of the reasons being that they were much older and in times gone by people had taken far more pride in the construction and attention to detail, just as in the outside world. It is not that these old houses were in any way masterpieces of art, or for that matter masonry, but the stones from which they were built were much better trimmed and fitted than those of modern times. But it did not signify any degeneration, as some would have it, but rather the loss of the art possessed by the first settlers, two of whom were masons by trade. With their passing away, and the deaths of their sons probably some fifty or sixty years ago, the highly skilled art has disappeared. In 1885 when the island adult male population was something not much above twenty souls, fifteen of these who put to sea in a lifeboat were drowned and never seen again and it is also possible that some skilled in the art of masonry vanished on this tragic occasion.

'Pointing' to the west, as they say, we passed well below the house of Bill and Lena Green, not the best house on the island by any manner of means. Bill was quite an old man bordering on seventy years of age and was known in his youth as an industrious man.

But Bill, after marriage so we were told, sunk lower and lower and became lazier and lazier. As the years passed the sheep he possessed and the quantity of potatoes he stored in his bins at the end of the digging season were almost negligible. If any family suffered the pangs of starvation it was his. There never was any hope for Bill. One missionary after another tried to help him but he always sank back to where he was before. In spite of all his faults he took his place at the oars with the other islanders and on birthdays his house was open like all the rest on the island to those who wished to call. As we passed we heard 'knock', 'knock', 'knock', coming from his miserable livingroom-kitchen and we knew what was going on because he was the butt of the islanders' humour.

They had noticed that Bill has started to board up his place again. 'It's the same old story, they say. Come winter time, an' you'se sure as I sit here an' old Bill will rip down his boardings for to burn! Then he'll have to start all over again same as 'e done before. It's the same old story. Some people prefer to burn they house down for firewood instead of doing an honest days work!'

But perhaps Bill this time made a better job of it and perhaps, with luck, his boarding and partitions would stand a couple of years.

We walked along the road that led some two miles further out to the Potato Patches. In the distance, towards the skyline, we saw another busy man, Frank Glass thatching his house.

We passed Rosa Rogers, a widow with a family of three, busily washing some clothes on the wonderful square slab of stone that many who lived in this vicinity used on their weekly wash day.

The method of scrubbing clothes on a stone was supposed to decrease their life by some 50%, if we were to believe some of the strangers who arrived at the island later on, but in a land where nothing else was available and where soap was scarce they had little other choice. Dirty clothes were beaten out on these slabs and I remember one missionary being upset probably with good reason when he noticed the Church altar dressings and his surplice being treated in the same manner by an otherwise well-meaning islander! Washing, scrubbing, sewing and cooking were amongst some of a Tristan woman's daily work.

In season they also helped their menfolk in the Potato Patches 'putting in', grubbing and digging out the potatoes when they were ready. Many women also accompanied the men to the other islands in order to try out the fat and cook for them when they were over there after petrels and wherever they went they took their knitting!

Paddy Rogers had married Laura Lavarello a year or two ago since when they have lived in the west end of Paddy's parent's comparatively large house. When Audrey was born, she cried and she cried and after a time Paddy realised it was time he made a move and built his own house. The rule on Tristan was that, after selecting a suitable site, one sought the Chief Islander's approval in case the site was not available. The owner then called hands to collect stone for the building; you then built your house until it was fit for habitation, and then got married. Paddy did things the other way around and got married first! Some were not fortunate to possess enough suitable wood with which to enable building to start. In those days, after a recent shipwreck, there was little delay; the Tristan maiden's prayer was said to be 'Please God send us a nice shipwreck so Johnnie can build a house and we can get married!'

Excavating a house site.

After the site has been chosen and approved, hands were called together, each man bringing his spade and pick and those who possessed such a valuable tool as a crow bar would be asked to bring that along too. The first job was excavating. All Tristan houses were sunk some two or three feet into the ground, at least, in order to get protection against the awful gales which swept the island in the winter months.

Fortune played a big part in the layout of a house in that the placing of the plateau and the perfect lie of the ground was such that it was natural to build the houses along the slope facing the sea with the advantage that the houses all faced downhill and hence had a good view in front of them. This not only gave the houses a north-north- westerly aspect facing the sea and sight of any shipping that might arrive at the island, but it also enabled the houses to face the midday sun and at the same time be gable-end on, east and west, to the prevailing winds with their strongest end meeting the gales.

The size of a house depended upon the size and quantity of wood they had available in the way of rafters, purlins and beams. Once decided, the size of the house was marked off with string and pegs in the excavated area. Usually young married couples could manage with a house some thirteen feet wide by thirty feet long, divided into a small bedroom at one end with the kitchen-cum-living

Building the east gable end of a new house.

room occupying the greater part of the other portion. As the family increased, and they collected more wood, the islanders did what they call 'stretch' their houses and move one end gable the requisite number of feet outwards and so added an extra room.

Usually only one kind of stone was used for the walls, back and front as well as gable ends, this being a soft type of volcanic rubble stone which could be easily sawn or chipped into blocks with the aid of an axe. With gun cotton, which they got from passing ships, they blasted a seam of this soft rock at the back of a district known as the Bog and carted it to the building site to be worked. This stone is known as volcanic tuff.

In a land where concrete was unknown foundations had to be made of another type of stone, also a volcanic conglomerate of grey stone with small white patches in it, which abounded on the Settlement plateau, sometimes above, but usually below, the surface. These round boulders were known locally as 'blue' stones and the heaviest obtainable were set in the ground to form the foundation, onto which the front and back soft stone walls were built up to the eaves. The gable ends, east and west, were constructed very broad at the base, for up the centre of one was the chimney flue, some twelve inches square. In the absence of cement the cracks between the blocks were filled in with loose stone and the

Cutting and sorting New Zealand flax for thatching.

final pointing was done on the outside with a mixture of wood ash and clay. This helped to keep out moisture but could not be used like concrete to carry any weight.

In the case of a house, as opposed to potato huts, wall plates were built in along the front and back walls, these being known on Tristan as the upper- and lower-side walls in preference to front and back. Likewise the islanders always talked of the east and west side of anything, no matter what it was, in preference to right and left.

In order to get the heavier stones up onto the gable ends two poles were placed, side by side, against the walls and the stones pushed up.

Naturally, to get the correct angle shape of gable end an old oar or shaft of wood was secured up the centre of the gable and a triangular piece of string stretched up the side, over the top of the pole and down the other to make a guide with which to build up the ends.

'Principals', made of pine, or failing that the largest trunks of island tree, were then bolted together at the apex and placed every four or five feet along the building with the butt ends secured to the wall plates. 'The rafting', likewise pine if it could be spared but far more often of island tree, were then nailed along the 'principals' and the whole was then ready for thatching.

Young married couples were far more interested in having a roof over their

Starting to thatch Reg Rogers' house.

heads and some protection from the winds than other refinements. Such things as floors, partitions walls and ceilings, or lofts as they called them, came by degrees after a time. Many started life with a mud floor and old newspapers plastered or nailed to the inside of the walls and these houses presented a picture of poverty and misery to those used to better things. But no matter who you were on Tristan everyone, down to the last man had started his married life in this humble state, with but a few sheep and probably no cattle at all. It was the industrious and intelligent islander who soon realised that there was room for much improvement and it was amazing, in a land of want, how soon, comparatively speaking, they eventually managed to board out their houses in a respectable manner. Boarding for walls and partitions often consisted of odd pieces of box wood of various sizes which had been thrown overboard by passing ships or in which the yearly stores from England or the Cape had been sent.

We sat down near Paddy's house and to eat our packed lunch of sandwiches.

Laurie, who had no tea at her parents-in-laws, arrived with Paddy's lunch and offered us a cup of cocoa which we gladly accepted. Paddy downed his axe and sat a few yards off on the stone he was trimming and we exchanged a few general remarks.

Paddy was Arthur Rogers' youngest brother but although we recognised a

Grass turfs finish the roof of the house.

fair family likeness, his character, demeanour and appearance we decided did in no way compare. Although a good-natured soul, and a man that I have no doubt would be prepared to sacrifice his life in an emergency, he did not promise at that stage to follow his brother's example. The great contrasts one found on Tristan in the various members of one family were strange. But the islanders knew no social or colour barriers and all lived happily together choosing, of course, their own particular friends.

As we turned east again retracing our tracks we passed the lower side east corner of Willie Lavarello's flax garden. We saw in the distance, at the bottom of Ned Green's, a gang of four men cutting flax for thatching. Two men were cutting with large knives, another two were tying it into bundles of a handy size, whilst two boys with donkeys were carting it up to Clara's where Frank Glass and a couple of hands were busily engaged in the important work. On the way for a closer view, however, we noticed that Chrissy's new potato hut was not yet complete, every house had its own in which the year's crop was stored in 'bins'.

We noticed that the huts were all built up and down, as the islanders would say, instead of being set parallel with the coastline, that is longwise with the back end sunk well into the ground on the 'upper side'! But the back gable and the two side walls were all built of blue stone in the manner of a loose stone

The home of Joseph and Elsie Glass and their family.

wall, with no fillings whatsoever between the stones. The walls, nevertheless were thick, perhaps eighteen inches, and we wondered how the rafters were supported as there were no wall plates. A close examination disclosed a most ingenious arrangement. Where the rafters met the walls, large pieces of soft stone had been built in and hollowed out to take the butt end of the rafters which, for rigidity, were both nailed into the soft stones and tied with wire. Purlins, as before, were spaced up and down each side and, where nails were not obtainable, were tied to the rafters with string and sometimes wire.

Window frames and uprights for doors were usually made and nailed to the soft stone walls after the thatch had been put on the roof and due to the absence of hinges the islanders made sliding box frame windows which of course were minus the usual cord, weight and pulley. The windows, when it was desired to admit fresh air, were either held up by friction, the wood swells often enough in the dampness, or they were kept open by a prop of wood, a wedge or a nail. Queen Mary once sent them a large quantity of plate glass from England and I believed they still had some left for building purposes. The total size of the windows was usually approximately two feet wide by three high, whereas doorways were three feet wide by six high, split in the centre stable fashion.

We found six men busy on Frank Glass's roof engaged in putting on a fresh thatch top, because his old one, which had been there some six or seven years, had started to leak in rainy weather. Frank had therefore called hands together the day before in the usual manner and Clara was busy inside doing her best to cook their dinner in the falling dust.

The best thatching material on Tristan was the indigenous grass known as tussock grass, common on islands in the Southern Ocean, and there was a time when it covered the island of Tristan da Cunha itself.

But, for some mysterious reason, it had almost completely vanished except in a few small gardens surrounding some of the houses. It is believed that the rats, which got ashore from the castaway barquentine *Henry A. Paull* in 1879, rapidly increased and multiplied and found the young shoots of the island tussock very palatable, with the result that it had almost completely vanished. Due to the very small quantity remaining, all privately owned, most people used New Zealand flax which was also grown in their gardens for the purpose. Flax was certainly introduced to the island, either from St. Helena or New Zealand, for none was to be found growing in a natural state on any of the island groups.

Three men were essential for one thatching gang. The thatcher sat on the roof with a 'needle', a large home-made flat piece of iron with a point on one end and a hole to take the hemp or yarn in the other, while his assistant stood under the roof inside the house, usually on the top of the loft or ceiling. His job was to take the needle as the thatcher pushed it through and thread it back again. The third member of the combination was the bundle thrower, who stood on the ground outside the house throwing readily-tied bundles of flax up to the thatcher, as required.

The islanders had developed team-work to a fine art in their thatching. Once it had started, and there was plenty of flax at hand, they worked until they were stopped either by their wives for the next meal or by darkness because they did not always get finished the back and the front in one day.

As we stood and watched we heard the rhythmic commands shouted by the thatcher and his assistant as the work proceeded.

"Bundle, nip, haul, up."

"Bundle, nip, haul, up," and so on, all day long.

When the thatcher was ready for his bundle, which was tied together with a small piece of yarn in the centre, the stalks all pointing the same way, he yelled out the first word of the sequence to the bundle thrower below who chucked it up to him without hesitation. This was placed, leaves downwards, closely against the last bundle to be secured, the needle pushed through the under row of flax round the outside of his new bundle, and his assistant inside grasped the needle as it appeared and pulled it gently through while in the meantime the thatcher was arranging his bundle so that it lay square and neatly in line. Then he gave the command 'nip', when the assistant pulled and held the yarn tight, at the same time poking the needle up through the centre of the new bundle back to the thatcher. He in turn grabbed the needle and pulled the cord tight and if his mate was not quick enough he would have his hand caught up in the yarn and have himself thatched to the roof with the flax! To avoid this the mate gave the thatcher the word 'haul' when he was ready and when, from his side, all was tight and ready for the next stitch, he informed the thatcher accordingly with his 'up'. The thatcher then knew that he could call for the next bundle and so it went on throughout the day until finished. Frank informed us that it took four hundred bundles of flax to thatch one side of his house or just over eight hundred to do his whole roof.

Once the thatching was completed the ridge along the top would not only look ugly with pieces of tussock or flax sticking out in all directions but rain would enter the centre and spoil anything that happened to be stowed away in the loft. The islanders finished their roofs with a row of grass turf from chimney to chimney which they cut from the grassy plateau in thickish sods. When freshly cut they presented quite an attractive appearance to their houses, with their red-grey gable ends and front walls, brown thatch, after it has dried out, and fresh green ridge turf. Sometimes, for a month or two, daisies blossomed along the ridge.

A chimney needed some sort of chimney pot, but in the absence of anything suitable the islanders hollowed a large slab of soft stone which was trimmed off square and placed over the flue to form a chimney.

If they had any paint to spare the door and window-frames were always the first to receive treatment. Some homes, when freshly painted in blue and white, looked quite attractive. Floorboards were never coloured as they were continually scrubbed but walls, fireplaces and ceilings would not be neglected if the opportunity offered a bright splash.

Bullock Carts

Making a ziz-zag course up hill we turned towards the westwards once more and passed the back of Christopher Swain's new house where we met three members of the Cyril Rogers family together with Gladys Swain as companion. They were returning from 'Old Bunt', a district, with two donkeys heavily laden with grass.

The grass, which was plucked from the mountainsides, where it grew thickest, was being carted home in string bundles to be tipped into the sheep pens to make manure. Throughout a certain time of year the men or boys drove the flocks of 'home' sheep to the Settlement with dogs to pen them up for the night to make manure which combined with the grass to fertilise their patches. Kelp was sometimes added, and the resultant rotting mixture was very strong and probably gave the island potatoes their lovely flavour.

Ellen told us that Cyril 'aint had his lunch yet. He got 'ome late an I went ter fetch 'im 'ome', so they did not tarry and neither did we because we saw Joe Repetto mending his cart and we were interested in what he was doing.

Apart from donkeys, which originally were reported to have been sent from St. Helena for the old hands in the early days of the Settlement, the only other island transport was by bullock cart, for all but a few of the islanders had never seen a horse in their lives.

Joe did not notice our approach and as we crept up unawares we snapped him busily engaged with a hand axe chopping a piece out of his axle in order to replacing the old rotten braces. Joe informed us that the cart could not be trusted to bear a heavy load 'without dropping it in the road' as he said.

"What do you call that long piece there, Joe?" we asked.

"The cart's pole," he replied rather amazed at our ignorance.

Tristanites were fond of the possessive genitive case in speech and always talked about the 'coat's pockets' or the 'kettle's cover', rather than the 'lid of the kettle' in preference to using 'of'.

"Where did you get such a nice long straight piece of wood like that, Joe?" my companion asked.

Loading a bullock cart with a large stone.

"I got that piece from Big Charlie Green a good many years back".

"Surely he didn't just give it you? Where did he get it from?"

"I guess it's a piece what wash up from South America or somewheres. He give it me for three small packets of baccy what I got out of a ship. The men ain't had a smoke for some time an' he wasn't was want it because he got his own pole so he let me have it for the baccy!"

"By Jove," I replied, "he must have been a fool to part with a piece of wood like that for tobacco!"

"Mr Crawford, when the men's hard up for baccy an' there ain't been a ship for a year or two, I guess some men would give the shirt off they backs for a fill of baccy."

We began to like Joe for he obviously was very much 'all there' and his facial features radiate intelligence and ability. He was a good carpenter and in spite of his shortage of tools managed to turn out excellent furniture once he 'gets' down to the job. We noticed he had a nice plane on his cart and assumed that this must have been borrowed from the Chief as there were only about two good planes on the whole island.

"And where did you get your wheels and axle?" we asked him, anxious to know the whole story in connection with the history of his cart.

"Them's pieces what come off driftwood. I dunno what h'island people would do if it wasn't for driftwood. One thing I do know, you'd never get your house built."

"What about the body, Joe, and where did you get the tyres?"

"The body's make out of h'odd bits of wood like boxwood an' packing cases, an' any old. bit of wood what you can lay a hold to. Them bands I got come off two big wheels what come off a ship".

We asked Joe to carry on working while we made a sketch.

The pole, which is eleven feet six inches long and about four inches in cross section, was secured to the axle by means of the pole bolt. Running out 'V' shape from either side of the centre of the pole to the axle to give rigidity were two stout pieces of wood known as 'braces', these were also bolted to both axle and pole. The small diameter wheels were made as solid as possible as the work the carts were expected to do up steep inclines and over stones and boulders soon smashed anything smaller. The thickness at the hub was approximately six inches, and the rim or band was three inches wide.

Due to the difficulty of obtaining wood of stout enough section to form the eighteen inch diameter wheels, these were usually made up in two or three parts, either bolted together with inset bolts or more often just spigotted together as shown. Without lathes the shaping of the wheels was a laborious task and this was generally done by chopping them to shape with an axe. The bands were bent in a forge and a splicing-piece joined the ends to make it circular. More work had to be done on the wheel itself, for it was unlikely at this stage that the band would fit on well. It was trimmed and, when still just a wee shade too big, it was hammered on and wedged so that it would not slip off. Bands were sometimes nailed into position to prevent them slipping but this often enough weakened the wheel.

It is as well that these people knew how to use a forge because they were dependent on a forge for the most important part of their carts, namely the 'arm'. This in reality was the axle itself about which the wheel revolves. If a round piece of iron was taken for the arm, one end had to be flattened and a hole bored through the centre to take the arm bolt, which secured it to the axle. A staple, likewise made from an odd bit of iron rod, prevented the arm from slipping off. Any fat or grease whatsoever was used as a lubricant for the wheels.

A strong beam called a cross piece was next bolted across the top of the axle, and extended almost the whole length. All that remained to complete the undercarriage, or rather, 'frame', was to fix the draw bolts and rubbing plates on the end of the pole.

We discovered that the body was made from box wood which was not a very complicated thing to make, the whole thing being built up on a framework called the bottom frame, with 6 staunchens and three rails forming the principal members. Boards were nailed round except for the back, which was made with loose piece to slide in and out called the 'tail boards'. These enabled manure and sand and other similar items to be shovelled out more easily.

The internal dimensions of the average cart were three foot six inches long, two feet two inches wide and about thirteen inches deep. The carrying capacity was therefore only seven cubic feet which was not very much. But Tristan carts were designed for one pair of oxen, and the loads they had to pull on the island probably compared favourably with the spans of the sixteen oxen we had sometimes seen in Southern Africa.

It is strange that the islanders never painted their carts even when they had paint to spare. I supposed that it soon wore off if they did so and, as carts were always kept out in the open, paint would not last very long.

A yoke was used to harness the oxen but Joe told us that he 'ain't got one here, but if you care to look on the wall back of Little Joe's I think you'll find one there that he borrows from Uncle Tom for to 'draw they's manure'.

We bid our agreeable host, who had tea sent out as per custom, of course, adieu and made our way to Little Joe Glass' to examine the yolk.

The construction of these was quite simple, dependent of course on the usual meagre necessities which were so hard to come by on Tristan. We noticed that the main part was just one beam of good wood slightly hollow in the centre and curved towards each end to take the neck of the oxen. Looped into complete semi-circles were the two bows made out of apple tree which were kept in position by a piece of string through holes near the ends. With iron plates on either side of the yoke to prevent wear, a hole was drilled to take a swivel eye through which passes the draw-ring. To yoke in the oxen first one bow was taken out and, with a bit of careful manoeuvring, this was placed under the neck of the appropriate beast. The yoke was then placed on top and the bow ends passed through their holes and tied. With one beast on one end and the yoke weighing hard down in the opposite direction, tending to twist the neck of the poor unfortunate animal, the mate was often likely to run off! An inexperienced boy yoking oxen might well smash the bow and loose the beasts. It was wise to have a second hand waiting with the mate to make the problems less difficult. With the oxen paired the draw ring was placed between the bolts on the pole and a crack of apple bough and rimpie whip would send them off in the right direction.

We were fortunate in that John the Baptist passed with his pair of bullocks yoked in, drawing a load of wood. He had been out to the Bluff that morning for the load he cut near Second Watron half way up to the Base. John the Baptist was a great sportsman with an attractive sense of humour and his reputation was such that if he couldn't find a joke in anything, he would make a joke and everyone would laugh. As he raised his cap by the peak with a good-natured smile we were at once at ease with him and offered him a cigarette.

"Thank you, Sir. I won't smoke all your cigarettes. I got some of me own self in my porcket what I got out of the last ship what come to the h'island, an' I guess I can offer you all one!. He! He! He!" he laughed.

We were compelled to laugh too because there is something very genuine about his happy-go-lucky manner that attracts us.

Cigarettes and tobacco were things which the islanders loved but seldom ever possessed except after the visits of a 'good' ship; and it was indeed not only strange but also funny that Johnnie was in the position to offer hospitality in that direction to us who, in an Islander's mind, were usually a spring or fountain of those valuable and soothing commodities.

My friend from the 'outside world' being a pipe smoker offered Johnnie his pouch and not being the least bit shy Johnnie could not resist the temptation of a practical joke.

"Thank you, Sir," he said and pocketed the pouch!

Poor Johnnie tried to keep a straight face for one second but could not.

"He! He! He! He!"

Johnnie's laughter was heard above everything else as he doubled up.

"I ain't going to have a smoke now thank you, Sir. I's late for my dinner an' I don't like to smoke just before I h'eat," he said eventually as he returned the pouch.

"We were going to ask you something about your oxen, Johnnie but if you are anxious to get home we won't delay you."

"That's all right, Sar, I aint in no hurry."

My friend asked him whose bullocks he was working.

"Them's my two bullocks, Night and Day" says he, pointing first at the brown one and then at the black.

We chatted to Johnnie about the island bullocks and finally said goodbye to him. I was to learn a lot more about these bullocks at a long session one evening at the house of Arthur and Martha. We noticed that, as Johnnie went by, his bullocks each had an identification split in the left and the right ear which was his mark.

John the Baptist Lavarello with his bullock cart drawn by Night and Day.

All cattle were privately owned. It was an islander's ambition to own a pair of oxen, preferably two pairs of oxen, which corresponded with our ambition to own a car, or perhaps two cars, in the 'outside world'. But by no means were all the islanders so fortunate. In good times perhaps a half to three quarters of the men might possess a pair and possibly half a dozen of the more industrious men a couple of pairs. Some on the other hand might have a share in a pair and others none at all.

When a young steer was born the owner naturally had to decide fairly soon whether he would let it run with the herd as a bull or whether he would cut it and train it as a draught ox. I should think that ninety-five times out of a hundred he decided to cut it, as to let it run was a dead loss to him personally. It was usually the custom to keep only two bulls with the home cattle and one or two at both Seal Bay and Stonyhill.

As the steers grew up the time came when they had to be broken in, and if they were wild they were left to roam for several days yoked in to the beast they would match, for bullocks always worked in pairs. They were seldom interchanged and only if one died did a stranger enter the yoke. Worked in pairs they likewise

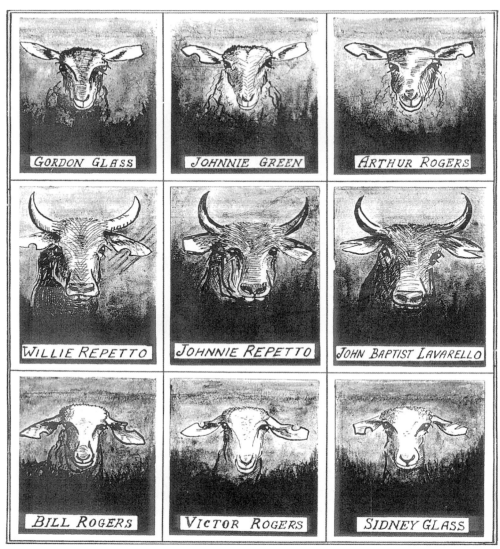

Livestock ear markings.

always stuck to the same side of the yoke because they got used to pulling one way and were more easily managed. A big crowd collected, at a safe distance, when it was known that someone was going to yoke in a wild steer and much amusement and laughter accompanied the escapades that followed. Sometimes they tossed a man and Frank Glass, the expert, had suffered many a fall.

After a few days the paired bullocks became used to one another and if they had not broken a couple of bows already it will be assumed that they were fairly safe. They were freed and yoked again. They were then given the cart to draw. Here again there were many amusing incidents and islanders had to organise the men to corner a run-away.

Most island bullocks had names which were used the whole time for manoeuvring the carts. Where they got them from I do not know. Some of the names were most attractive and many pairs were named using the same initial letters. Others were opposites, like John the Baptist's, Night and Day. Some of the interesting and picturesque names were:

Bat and Ball	Lock and Line	Spark and Star
Bank and Bay	Derby and Duke	Lark and Linnet
Buck and Berry	Right and Left	Night and Day
Orange and Blue	Nep and Sandy	Jerry and Tom
Broad and Diamond		

Spot and Berry (Buck, who was yoked with Spot, probably died)

Many bullocks were called the same names, that is, a couple of men may have each possessed a pair called Lock and Line, a combination that seemed to be the most common. If one steer died a new one was yoked in with the still-living mate and often named after the deceased.

Many of the men engaged on other types of jobs and who were on their way home in the middle of the day had started something else by the afternoon. We saw Arthur Rogers just below his house back from his wood-fetching on Little Beach that morning. He had called together a couple of hands to work on the new boat mast they were making. This was a spar over twenty feet long which Thomas had found one day washed up on one of the beaches. As the finder he had first claim and decided to use it for the boat which he, Arthur, Ned Green and Reginald shared, among a few others.

When I saw them carry up this thick timber I wondered how on earth they would cut it down to half its diameter, for as it stood it was far too thick. In the absence of tools I think I would have fought shy of the job and waited for the day when perhaps something more suitable might drift ashore. But not these men. Four of them had spent nearly three quarters of the day chipping away at the thing with ordinary hand axes, and I was amazed at the well-proportioned tapered result of their labours. Some idea of the work involved could be judged by the large pile of chippings which could be seen under the spar, as they call it. It was only when they had nearly completed the job that Arthur's valuable steel plane was produced to even the surface. These men were indeed to be admired for the difficult tasks they tackled. They finished their spar by 5 o'clock that day.

As the day drew to a close we were tiring and felt that the time had come for us to depart. We had visited many and learnt a lot, but we had only seen between twenty to thirty people engaged in their daily work, many belonging to the same families. There were over fifty families on the island and you can be sure that the balance of the population were just as busily engaged in various other activities as those with whom we spoke. We had remained in the Settlement but many went out two miles away to their patches to work their ground. Others went off fishing and others will have stayed behind to make moccasins and do all the other hundred and one odd jobs which had to be done.

Bullock carts make their way from the Settlement to the Potato Patches two miles away.

Family Tree

The community on Tristan consisted of two hundred and twenty-five souls in whose veins flowed the blood of their English, Scotch, Irish, American, Dutch, Italian, Cape and St. Helena forefathers.

They were a perfectly average community consisting, like all other communities, of good and mediocre, intelligent and shy, clean and neglected, industrious and indolent people and almost any other contrast one may care to think about. Only seven of whom had ever been to the outside world. The remaining two hundred and eighteen had lived in the middle of the South Atlantic all their lives and had never sailed away.

There were approximately fifty-two families, but only seven family surnames; Glass, Green, Hagan, Lavarello, Repetto, Rogers and Swain. The population is descended from shipwrecked sailors, soldiers and others who have elected to remain on the island in preference to the 'outside world'.

The settlement on Tristan da Cunha was established as a community in the year 1816 when Corporal Glass, his wife and family and a couple of masons, decided to spend the rest of their lives there carrying on a lucrative exchange of seal skins and whale oil with passing sealers.

In 1827 five bachelors, of European descent, desired wives and placed a request before the captain of a passing sailing ship that next time he called could he produce a companion for each single man. Five St. Helena women, some thousand miles away to the north, volunteered to undertake the great adventure and were taken to Tristan to marry their unknown husbands.

It is interesting that the would-be wives were very carefully selected and the primary considerations were good character and absence from disease. The then Governor of St.

Helena, General Walker, took a personal interest in this proposition and it was with his blessing that the five young damsels sailed to their new home and their unseen husbands-to-be. The story goes that when they were landed on the beach at Tristan each man chose a girl to his liking without clashing with any of his mates and they lived happily ever after. The way one man chose his bride even before he saw them is worthy of record: 'The first old hen what step out of the boat I's going to kop 'er for my wife!' said one of the pioneers in the general excitement and tension that preceded the happy day, and fate must have arranged the right lady to tread on the black sandy beach, for sure enough he married her and the story is still told today on the island.

Since that date, with the exception of the introduction of fresh blood in the nature of castaways and runaways from passing ships who decided to remain on the island and make it their home, the population was left to intermarry and breed to their heart's content but not with uncontrolled promiscuity.

From the day the original settlers arrived until today, marriage has been most sacred amongst them and the very foundation of their existence, although it would not be true to say that there have never been any illegitimate births. One on record was the result of a shipwrecked sailor's few months sojourn on the island whereas the origins of two others is unknown. A total of three over one hundred and thirty years with an island population throughout that period of one to two hundred persons is by no means excessive and compares favourably with any other community similarly situated throughout the world.

There was however a great deal of inter-marriage, for due to the isolation of this lonely outpost it was impossible for them to acquire wives of any origin but their own. One of the objects of the Norwegian Scientific Expedition's work at Tristan da Cunha in 1937-38 had been to try to discover how far, if at all, this intermarriage had been detrimental to the community, and if so, in what direction.

After four months of very close study by a doctor and sociologists, and a thorough medical and sociological survey, they were convinced that intermarriage has had no detrimental effect upon the community. Any shortcomings they displayed in such matters as shyness, slowness of speech and ignorance of certain matters which we of the outside world took as a matter of course, could in no way whatsoever be attributed to intermarriage but rather natural causes as the result of their lack of education and isolation.

From a medical point of view the population was fit, strong and healthy and the men were as strong as oxen. Fate has decreed a hard life for the Tristan islanders and although most were busy in one way or another every day, they made good use of their own time and took a day off when they so desired. They bore loads twice as heavy as many of us and would back loads that soldiers shunned. As regards their teeth, they were reputed to be the best in the world. It was true that some islanders suffered badly in the winter from asthma and one or two have at times been so 'tight chested', as they called it, that if it hadn't been for the presence of a doctor in their midst in 1942-46, they most certainly could have succumbed. This was accounted for by the unfortunate fact that two of the original settlers, one from Europe and the other a woman from St. Helena, were also sufferers and as this was hereditary, it has been handed down from generation to generation.

Such things as chicken pox, whooping cough and other illnesses were things quite unknown on Tristan and the inhabitants led very healthy lives throughout the year. The exception was 'island sickness', a form of diarrhoea, which mysteriously affected many some time during the summer months, but after a bout they were free for the rest of the year and it did not follow that it recurred the following year.

A strange fact in connection with the islanders' health was that when a ship from the Cape arrived at the island and made contact with the local inhabitants practically the entire population went down with colds and coughs during the next two weeks. When the coughs vanished they never returned until the next ship. A ship that had sailed direct from England was said to have been at sea for so long that the germs it may have carried had died on the way and did not threaten their health in this way. It is thought that due to their isolation they probably had very little resistance to diseases and that if a ship did arrive at the island with such a disease as chicken pox, it might very well have disastrous consequences and possibly many of the islanders might succumb.

The islanders suffered, although not through physical pain, from intestinal worms which, according to Dr Woolley, Medical Officer in charge, 1942-1944, was the result of geese and livestock walking in the island water supply and introducing germs which islanders subsequently drank in water. After I left I understand that he made an organised clearing of these worms with doses of medicine. The 'return' in most cases was most alarming with some women having fifty of these in their stomach, whereas others had none!

With regard to their teeth, various theories existed as to the cause of the perfection, many holding that the scarcity of sugar and sweetmeats was the prime contributing factor. Others maintained that the excellence of their water supply was the cause as the stream which flowed down the east side of the Settlement emerged as a spring at the foot of the cliffs. A third school of thought was that the life they lead is the life of a seafarer and a farmer combined, the ideal outdoor existence vital for perfect health.

From a sociological point of view, the islanders were reasonably well-informed about their own affairs. To listen to an island conversation, without causing embarrassment, told you at once that, when these people were together in their natural surroundings discussing matters of mutual interest, they talked as fast as could be expected. Small wonder that, when these people were in surroundings quite alien to their lives, such as the cabin or mess room of a ship, with electric lights, taps or radios around them, these people were slightly ill at ease and inclined to say 'Yes, Sar' to any question placed before them! But they were not as bad as that, although some visitors to the island departed convinced that these were primitive folk!

It was therefore quite clear that although intermarriage at quite an alarming rate had taken place on Tristan for the past one hundred years, it had had no detrimental effects on them and dispelled popular theories to the contrary!

I was struck with the idea of trying to work out the whole Tristan da Cunha family tree, for as the older hands were dying off, so some very valuable information was being lost in connection with their forefathers. This had never been done before and the road lay open for some very interesting investigation. To go back two or three generations was something that I could do almost with my eyes shut but the further back one went so the more difficult the problem became.

I set off with pencil and pad and called on many of the oldest inhabitants in search of what was to be uncovered. My problems were many. Some had forgotten their grandparents first names and others never knew them! Tact of the highest order was needed for if a statement was placed before them, such as 'Was your grandmother's name Sarah', ten-to-one they would at first agree, eager to satisfy without giving the proposition much thought. Tactics therefore of a different nature had to be devised and questions placed in a round about way.

Having a good idea of their background was a great help. I think it is true to say that I probably knew more about their history than they themselves knew. I also made use of the islander's popular Christian names or nicknames.

Little Sam Swain, for instance, has the Christian name of Robert but no one on the island with the possible exception of himself and his own little family knew who Robert Swain was. On the other hand all knew 'Little' Sam Swain from 'Old' Sam, although 'Little' Sam is a large man of seventy, whereas 'Old' Sam is a smaller man approaching ninety! Sometimes, in order to get one small piece of information, such as 'had Sarah Rogers a brother called Tom', I had to sit drinking a cup of tea for an hour before the necessary information could be obtained. It took me two months, working intermittently, to get the tree shipshape.

It was often necessary to feel my way very carefully by talking quite naturally about completely different things to discover the answer without the islanders knowing what I had been after. I first of all dealt with each family name and worked right back to the original settlers. 'Bala' used to go out Jinny's where she kept a school for the children', someone innocently said during a conversation about the teaching of their forefathers to read and write. At such statements I cocked my ears with interest.

Who was 'Bala' and was Jinny one of Corporal Glass's children? So my tree grew and grew until it was completed. As pieces of information trickled in so I gleefully entered the name on my tree. There were no text books or any published works on which to rely, a fact which made things more difficult. Then I went on, studying marriages and inter-relationships, so the various families were pieced together. Eventually my excitement and satisfaction was complete when I discovered that, by the marriage of Thomas Glass of the second generation to Mary Swain, the whole island down to the very last man and woman were all inter-related or connected into one large family tree!

A study of the original tree revealed some most interesting things. I had divided them up into generations, and the first thing which caused a headache was the fact that Pieter Groen, in future known as Peter Green, the castaway Dutchman who married Mary Jacobs of St. Helena, although a man of the first generation on Tristan married a girl whose mother Sarah Jacobs was also of the first generation! Mother and daughter arrived at the island at the same time and eventually both married original settlers and were therefore both of the same generation. In a way, this was not strictly true and some maintained that Peter Green was a second generation man, but I was only interested in Tristan and the islander's genealogical history.

Peter Green arrived at the island in 1836, only eight years after the wives were introduced so he can safely be called an original settler. Mary Jacob's father was a man from, not necessarily of, St. Helena and never came to Tristan. Her mother, Sarah Jacobs who brought her to Tristan, married the original settler Thomas Hill Swain of Hastings, England. Families of those days were very large. Thomas and Sarah Swain produced twelve children and Peter and Mary eight. Alexander Cotton who was reported to have kept guard over Napoleon at St. Helena came to Tristan in 1821. His St. Helena wife, Maria whose surname was unknown, produced a family of thirteen. The Cotton family had died out from Tristan in name, but many of the present islanders possessed Cotton blood.

THE TRISTAN DA CUNHA FAMILY TREE

DIAGRAM TO SHOW THE ORIGINAL
SETTLERS AND THE MALE
DESCENDANTS THROUGH WHOM
THE FOREFATHERS OF THE PRESENT
ISLANDERS CAN BE TRACED.

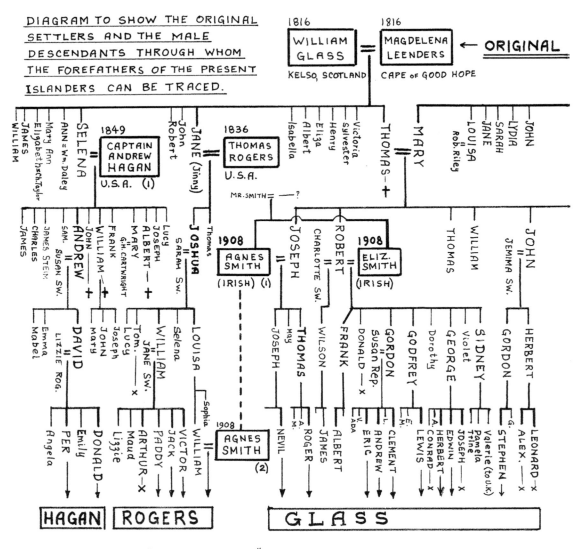

1. SETTLERS FROM "OUTSIDE WORLD" SHOWN IN RECTANGLES.
2. BROTHERS (AND SISTERS, WHERE GIVEN) ARE NOT SHOWN IN SEQUENCE OF BIRTH.
3. FAMILIES WHO EMIGRATED ARE NOT SHOWN.
4. 15 MEN WHO LOST LIVES IN 1885 BOAT DISASTER SHOWN THUS: †

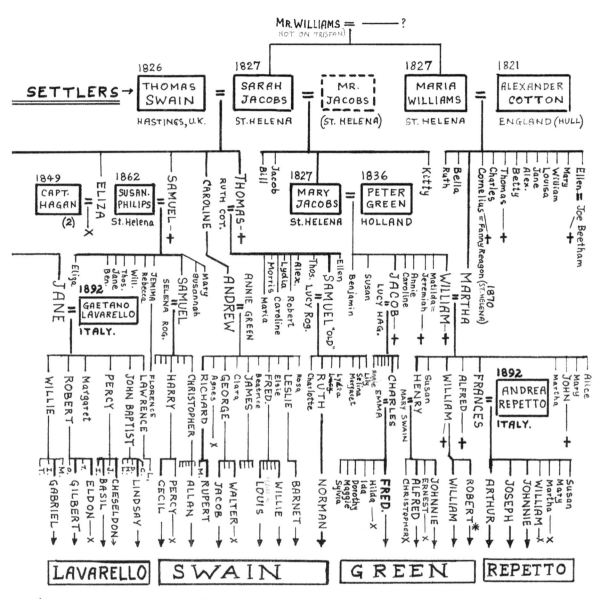

MR. WILLIAMS = ———— ?
(NOT ON TRISTAN)

SETTLERS →

| 1826 THOMAS SWAIN | = | 1827 SARAH JACOBS | = | 1827 MR. JACOBS | 1827 MARIA WILLIAMS | = | 1821 ALEXANDER COTTON |

HASTINGS, U.K.   ST. HELENA   (ST. HELENA)   ST. HELENA   ENGLAND (HULL)

1849 CAPT. HAGAN (2)
ELIZA = X
1862 SUSAN. PHILIPS — St. Helena
SAMUEL +
CAROLINE
RUTH COT.
THOMAS +
Jacob
Bill
1827 MARY JACOBS — St. HELENA
= 1836 PETER GREEN — HOLLAND
Kitty
Ruth
Bella
1870 Cornelius = Fanny Reagon (ST. HELENA)
Charles +
Thomas —
Betty
Alex.
Jane
Louisa
William
Mary
Ellen = Joe Beetham

JANE
Elise.
Ben.
Jane
Thos.
Will.
Rebecca
JEMIMA
SELENA ROG.
SAMUEL
Mary
Susannah
ANDREW
ANNIE GREEN
Morris
Caroline
Maria
Lydia
Robert
Alex.
Thos. Lucy Rog.
SAMUEL "OLD"
Ellen
Benjamin
Susan
LUCY HAG.
JACOB +
Caroline
Annie
Jeremiah
Matilda =
WILLIAM +
MARTHA
Alice
Martha
John
Mary
Susan

1892 GAETANO LAVARELLO — ITALY.
1892 ANDREA REPETTO — ITALY.

WILLIE
ROBERT
Margaret
PERCY
JOHN BAPTIST
LAWRENCE
FLORENCE
HARRY
CHRISTOPHER
RICHARD
Agnes
GEORGE
Clara
JAMES
Beatrice
FRED.
Elsie
LESLIE
Rosa
Charlotte
RUTH
Margaret
Lily
Selina
Annie EMMA
CHARLES
MARY SWAIN
HENRY
Susan
WILLIAM
ALFRED
FRANCES
ROBERT *
ARTHUR +
JOSEPH
JOHNNIE

GABRIEL
GILBERT
ELDON — X
BASIL
CHESELDON →
LINDSAY
CECIL
PERCY — X
ALLAN
M. RUPERT
JACOB
WALTER — X
LOUIS
WILLIE
BARNET
NORMAN
Sylvia
Maggie
Dorothy
Ida
Hilda — X
FRED.
CHRISTOPHER X
ALFRED
ERNEST — X
JOHNNIE
WILLIAM
ROBERT *
ARTHUR +
Martha
William
Mary
Susan

| LAVARELLO | SWAIN | GREEN | REPETTO |

↓ = DESCENDANTS INTO 6TH GENERATION.
(1) = FIRST MARRIAGE.   (2) = SECOND MARRIAGE.
X = NO ISSUE.
DATES ABOVE RECTANGLES ARE DATES OF ARRIVAL.

COMPILED BY
Allan B. Crawford.
1946 & 1979

Alexander Cotton and Maria's child Martha of the second generation married William Green, son of Peter, likewise of the second generation, and thus in the early days the Greens, Cottons, and Swains were related through Sarah Jacobs.

Andrea Repetto, an Italian castaway who arrived at the island in 1892, decided to stay on the island and by marrying Frances Green daughter of William, so the family of Repetto merges into this great branch. On the other side was the original settler, Corporal William Glass from Kelso, Scotland, with his original settler wife, of Cape coloured origin, who came to the island with him in 1819(?) and they produced the grand figure of sixteen children. One of the children, Selena, married an American sealer, Captain Hagan who remained on the island until his death, and they produced a large family of eleven children.

Corporal Glass and Lena's Thomas was the only male to perpetuate their name on the island. Of their six children, Jane married the Italian sailor companion of Repetto, called Lavarello, and so fresh blood is introduced into this branch. But that was not all, for there was yet one more name to be recorded.

Sometime, about the middle of the last century, Thomas Rogers, an American engaged in the sealing trade, took a fancy to another of Corporal Glass' children Jinny (Jane) and decided to marry her and remain on the island for the rest of his life. They only had a small family consisting of two boys, Thomas, who left the island and never returned, and Josuah, who married a Tristan girl from whom the Rogers family were descended.

This process of interbreeding intensified and reached a stage when every child on the island, and nearly all their parents too, were all descended from Sarah Jacobs of St. Helena.

As time went on, people did not always marry into their own generation with the result that many interesting relationships could be discovered from the family tree. An expert would probably have discovered far more but I was able to extract a few interesting facts, such as the family of Fred Green and Alice Green, who married and had three children, Benjamin, Barton and Martha.

Martha was my godchild, as she was born while I was on Tristan da Cunha as a member of the Norwegian Scientific Expedition. The children, Benjamin, Barton and Martha were their own second cousins, they were also, through another branch in their family, second cousins once removed in the Green branch. In the Glass-Rogers branch, however, they were their own third cousins once removed. Tracing these three children to the Swain branch and I found that they were their own fourth cousins, twice over!

From the family tree the ancestors of every person on Tristan da Cunha could be traced right back to the original settlers. It was also possible to trace back many who had left the island but there was no point in further investigation.

The question as to whether intermarriage produced, or tended towards, sterility in a closed community like Tristan was also a matter for discussion and one hundred and thirty years was rather a short time for application here. Since the early 1800s the size of each family had dropped off at a very great rate, but that was common throughout the world.

The generations on Tristan could be split up quite nicely from the foundation of the Settlement in 1816 up to the present day with approximately each generation corresponding to 20 years difference. Actually this was not exact but fitted in very nicely in the Swain family starting at 1820 for the first generation.

The table below shows only the descendants of the original, first generation settlers, showing: the decade; the appropriate generation; the total number of people in that generation of all families except those who left Tristan; the number of separate families which go to make up these totals; the average size of family per generation.

Year	Generation	Total of that generation	No. of Families	Average Size of Family
1820	1st	-	-	-
1840	2nd	40	3	13
1860	3rd	52	7	7
1880	4th	61	12	5
1900	5th	88	25	3
1920	6th	50	13	4
1940	7th	13	5	3

The most numerous generation was the 5th but with the departure of seventy persons to the Cape and the United States around 1856 and various other similar emigrations from time to time between 1880 and 1900, not to forget the awful boat disaster in 1885 when fifteen out of the total of eighteen men on the Island were drowned in one day, considerable havoc was caused with analyses of this kind; but this was the best that could be done under the circumstances.

Such names as Riley, Beetham, White, Johnson and Miller, well known on Tristan many years ago and often connected with the island's past history, did not enter into my study. They had lived all their lives, or emigrated from, Tristan in the last century which meant that their blood line had disappeared from the island.

A great deal could said for the Tristan people, their character and their appearance as there was on record a large percentage of islanders who had married sailors from Europe and settled elsewhere, mostly in the Cape, England, United States and Australia. Of the islanders at this time, Mrs Frances Repetto, the head woman, had the largest number of descendants in seven children, twenty-seven grandchildren and eleven great-grandchildren. The numbers of grandchildren and great-grandchildren were growing, and I had a report of the birth of one of each, which I included in the above figures. Mrs Repetto was seventy years of age in 1945, with seven nephews and nieces, twenty-five great-nephews and nieces and approximately ten great-great nephews and nieces. The latter figure was growing almost monthly!

It was a fact that on Tristan that no woman had ever died in childbirth. From the early part of the last century a couple of women learnt, probably through necessity and by experience, all that was necessary for them to know and that has been handed down through the generations up till the present day when something like half a dozen women were capable of dealing with the situation. There were no doctors or midwives on hand.

I heard from a nursing sister who was a member of the 1942-43 naval establishment that their methods, when compared with the outside world, left much to be desired; their idea of cleanliness and germs did not coincide with modern procedures. When a girl on Tristan was due for delivery, she decided for herself which midwives she would have at her bedside and, a few days before, would probably go herself, or send someone, to 'call' them in advance for the great event. Sometimes two would suffice, at other times three or even four might be 'called'.

The family tree revealed that it was a very rare thing indeed for islanders to marry and be without offspring. The only two of whom I was aware were Tom Rogers and Rebecca Swain, both of the third generation, and Arthur Rogers and Martha Repetto, both of the fourth generation. I did not discover anything about Tom and Rebecca as she died long before I ever visited Tristan, but in the case of my good friends, Arthur and Martha, I knew that in her youth she used to have pains and the doctor of the *R.Y.S. Quest*, which visited the island on an expedition in 1922, advised her against having any family.

There was an understanding on Tristan that the bigger your family the easier would be your declining years, for in a land where money was unknown and wealth was dependent upon the work put into the ground every year, to have a few healthy young boys and girls around at digging and spading time was an asset not to be despised.

From as many different sources as possible, such as ships' reports and the like, I made a careful study of the total population since the foundation of the settlement. A graph between total population on the vertical axis and time on the horizontal showed some very remarkable things. From 1810, when the population was two, up until 1827, when the five women were introduced from St. Helena, the sluggish rate of increase was a figure of about one person per year for fifteen years. Suddenly, as children were born to the St. Helenans, the rate went up to three persons per year for the next sixteen years, a rate of increase of three times what it was previously.

But that was not to be wondered at as in the early days there were only two women on the island until the arrival of the wives from across the water. And so without control from 1827 to 1856, the number of inhabitants increased at this alarming rate until the arrival of Reverend Taylor, from the Society for the Propagation of the Gospel, in 1851. In those comparative days of plenty, when sealers and whalers used to call for fresh meat, water and potatoes; when many of the islanders were able to barter sea elephant oil; when skimmed milk could be fed to the pigs and butter appeared at the table three times daily; their lot was nevertheless so hard that the Revd Taylor managed, in 1856, to induce 25 people to leave for a better existence.

A year later a further forty five departed for the Cape area of South Africa, this left but thirty one on the island, and it was his one regret that he could not take these away too! But for the thirty one left behind, comparative prosperity returned once more and once again the population was left to take on its natural rate of increase. Between 1856 and 1880 the islanders were once more without a parson or anyone to educate their children. Upon the arrival of Reverend Dodgson, brother of the famous Lewis Carroll, in 1880, the population had surpassed by nine the 'dangerous' figure of one hundred. With so many people scratching a meagre existence it was not long before he was able to induce several batches of people to leave. Letters were exchanged between the British Admiralty, the British Government in the Cape and the S.P.G. and it was possible by bartering their services aboard ship along with a stock of fresh meat and vegetables to obtain a passage and sail away from the island to a better and more pleasant land beyond the horizon. Between 1880 and 1902 several islanders left in this way.

In 1885 fifteen men were lost at sea in a tragic manner. The men, in dire need of provisions, put out to a passing sailing ship which hove in sight, and for which purpose the fifteen men crewed a new lifeboat. It had been presented to them by the British Government in recognition for their services in rescuing the castaways of the British ship *Shakespeare*, which was wrecked off Inaccessible Island in 1883.

These fifteen men, twelve of whom were married, were last seen close to the ship *West Riding* and were then shut out from view. The *West Riding* reported upon arrival in Australia, that she last saw the boat several miles astern and thinking the men might not get back to the island, reported that she cruised around in the vicinity searching for them without success before departing for Australia. Those men were never seen again, nor was any trace of evidence found, as the islanders combed the beaches in vain for pieces of wreckage. The names of those who vanished in the lifeboat were:

Name	Relationship to the former	Family left on the island
Thomas Glass	-	Wife and 6 children
William Green	connected by marriage	Wife and 10 children
Jacob Green	Brother	Wife and 7 children
Jeremiah Green	Brother	Wife and 1 child (?)
John Green	Nephew	-
Billy Green	Brother	Wife and 2 children
Alfred Green	Brother	-
Cornelius Cotton	Uncle	Wife and 5 children
Thomas Cotton	Brother	-
Joe Beetham	Brother-in–law to Cotton	Wife and 8 children
Billy Hagan	Connected by marriage	Wife and 3 children
Albert Hagan	Brother	-
John Steen Hagan	Brother	-
Sam Swain	Uncle	Wife and 11 children
Thomas Swain	Brother	Wife and 9 children

It is a mystery which will forever remain unsolved, one can imagine the terrible mental suffering and torment to the loved ones left behind! The fate of their menfolk was unknown. Had they perhaps been taken on board the *West Riding* and sailed away to some other land? Perhaps they had been tempted by the captain to seek new homes in a land flowing with milk and honey, perhaps to some lonely pacific island.

But the islanders could not believe that the men would be so callous. For years the women waited in vain, thinking that some day one of the fifteen might repent and send word back to his home in the Atlantic. But nothing was ever heard. This loss was a serious blow to the island, which was left with nothing more than a community of helpless weeping women and children. With the exception of one man Samuel Swain, who was the oldest inhabitant and alive to tell the tale in 1945, there was not a normal man of adult age left on the island.

Of the three men on the Island of which Samuel was one, one was reputed to be insane while the other went mad and had to be placed in a straight jacket. There were only enough boys left on the Island to man a small boat which itself was said to be in a very 'shaky' condition.

As their only friend in the outside world, and as the only man who really knew the island and its folk, Revd Dodgson, upon hearing of the terrible calamity returned for a further three years. Other groups were induced to leave as the opportunity arose from time to time.

They were the male members of what really amounted to one large family, for those who were not blood relations one to the other were connected by marriage. This was a tragedy that was to influence and affect the whole Island for many years to come.

In 1903, when the population was sixty one, further efforts were made from the Cape of Good Hope to enable all of the inhabitants to emigrate. However, as these efforts were dependent on the whole community being involved, the offer was withdrawn when a unanimous decision was not forthcoming. During

The men, in their Sunday best, chat and smoke after the morning church service.

the next forty years or so the rate of increase in the population reverted to its original level of between three or four a year, the total having risen to one hundred and eighty three in 1942.

The beginning of the twentieth century marked the universal acceptance of the steamship and, as year succeeded year and decade, sailing ships became more and more uncommon and seldom visited the island. Sailing ships often offered easier facilities for taking on extra hands enabling the islanders to emigrate with greater ease. But now steamers, with their refrigeration spaces and modern methods of storing fresh water had forgotten this outpost which years ago was of such valuable assistance to them on their long voyages.

The fact that every member of the crew usually has his own specified job assigned to him and did not need extra hands contributed towards the present day impossibility for islanders to leave for better lands. Other drawbacks were regulations preventing the movement of the people of this world from one country to another without registration and passports. As no such items existed at Tristan they were quite powerless to leave as immigration problems at ports of arrival also hindered their entry into foreign lands.

Richard Swain and son, Rupert, proudly display their catch. Crawfish at their feet, five-fingers in the foreground and mackerel, snoek and steenbras.

Seeds of Doubt

Tristan da Cunha was not the place for the visit of an intellectual conversationalist. The islanders knew practically nothing of the 'outside world'. From the chance meeting of sailors of different nationalities who had called in passing ships, perhaps not so frequently as once a year, they learnt that there were people such as Americans, Frenchmen, Norwegians, and the like. But what exactly all these different nationalities meant, and how they all fitted into the political sphere of things, the islanders naturally had not much idea.

On the other hand, in connection with their own affairs they knew nearly all that they could be expected to know. They knew the weather sequences at the island and when it was safe to sail across the twenty miles of open South Atlantic Ocean which separated them from the islands they visited yearly in search of sea birds, their eggs and guano. They knew how to make thirty foot canvas boats out of driftwood, packing cases and old ships' sails. Every man was his own farmer, fisherman, carpenter and house builder. Those who had been lucky and had managed to collect good quality wood had been able to board out their houses. Others had made bullock carts and spinning wheels with a bare sufficiency of tools.

Of course, there were a few lazy ones, mediocre farmers and others who preferred to kill off sheep until they had none left, rather than do an honest day's work in their potato patches. These were the islanders whose potatoes were all eaten up by June or July and for the remaining five months of the year they and their children were close to starvation. Fortunately they were a small minority. But it was unfair to judge any community by its worst members. It was not they who were characteristic of Tristan, quite the reverse!

As outsiders it seemed to us that the islanders could make better us of their ground if they were more industrially inclined and grew large quantities of vegetables to supplement their otherwise monotonous diet of fish and potatoes. It is true that their diet was varied in season, and from time to time by beef and mutton, but potatoes were consumed for breakfast, lunch, and supper almost every single day of the year, with practically no other variation in the vegetable line, except for an occasional pumpkin in season.

But the growing of vegetables on Tristan was all but an impossible task on account of the large number of factors working against the enthusiast. Our better instincts should have told us that if it were so easy, human nature being what it is to take the line of least resistance, they would have been prompted in their own interests to plant seeds, let them grow and satisfy their gastric instincts with delicious vegetables.

Soon after our arrival we each decided to show these men what could be done, for, unlike them, we had seeds to the value of £50 and all the tools needed for the job. The Doctor and the Padre, both of whom were practical men with a store of knowledge in many things including horticulture and agriculture, the leading Telegraphist, Supply Assistant and many more, including myself, constructed gardens in various places on the island and planted seeds of all descriptions with great enthusiasm.

Some of us, I regret to say, were almost spiteful in our enthusiasm and longed in a few weeks to show the islanders just how indolent they were but they chuckled amongst themselves at the Settlement and repeated the old island story, namely that 'Strangers who come to the island always think they know best in such matters'. Nevertheless, they decided to co-operate and lend assistance but were inwardly convinced that before long we would learn our lesson just as others had done in the past.

The Doctor started near his residence. After almost complete failure, judging by 'outside world' standards, he renewed efforts and constructed gardens in a sheltered gulch known as Knockfolly Gulch, situated about three quarters of a mile from the Settlement. Again, after many weeks of toil, he had nothing to show from his multi-various rows of seeds!

Next came the Padre, who with the help of some of the more intelligent islanders made a garden in Big Watron, a small gulch on the east side of the Settlement through which flows the island water supply. About all that could be shown after several weeks of toil was a row of parsley. I had my own patches, disused potato patches which I had acquired from an islander in 1938, a mile and a half from the village in a district known as the Valley. Here I planted row upon row of cabbages, onions, cauliflowers, beets, potatoes and even strawberries.

And what happened? Doctor's garden was too exposed and gales, which were wont to sweep the island many times a year, blighted his seedlings in one night just at a time when they appeared to be thriving so well. His Knockfolly

Some of the potato patches, two miles from the Settlement.

Gulch garden was broken into by sheep and what they missed, caterpillars and rats finished off. Most of Padre's garden was washed away by a flood which followed a heavy downpour of rain, and what few areas the water spared had to be abandoned. As for my patches 'out the Valley', wind, rats, grubs, hens, white flies and floods did their ravaging work in turn. In spite of constant grubbing out of twelve rows of potatoes my yield was barely five bushels.

Ironically enough, these five bushels came in useful for the feeding of one of my godchildren, the child of a poor and not altogether industrious family, during the lean winter months. Out of three or four rows of cabbages, only four plants came to heads, miserable balls of grub-eaten leaves about the size of my fist! Nevertheless, I was able on one or two occasions to bring back with me to the Naval Station a sack of cabbage greens which under the circumstances were better than the tinned variety upon which we otherwise depended.

However, compared with the work put into the ground and the quantity of seeds planted, these crops were few, uneconomical and all but a waste of time.

We had failed and our criticism of the islanders had been proven unjust. We had 'found out' for ourselves, and just as they had smiled when we started they were now entitled to turn around and say 'we told you so'.

An attempt to grow vegetables on Tristan da Cunha was then, one vicious circle of misfortune and disappointment. If it was not a gale, with wind velocities of perhaps eighty miles an hour, it was rats. If they have been otherwise occupied, perhaps out at the patches eating your potatoes, and if sheep and donkeys had not succeeded in breaking down the loose stone walls, it would be 'grubbing' time and a million caterpillars would be eating the plants, just as fast as they could killed off with you fingers.

Every morning around Christmas time gangs of men and women went out in an attempt to exterminate these pests. Nevertheless their efforts were productive and those who treated 'grubbing' lightly suffered from potato shortages the following winter.

The islanders did not spray their potatoes as they did not have any unlimited quantities of poison spray nor the right type of contact in the Cape to keep them supplied. They were thwarted by lack of money to purchase the necessary items and the absence of regular communications in the past has also contributed to the general hopelessness of the situation.

Windbrakes were to a certain extent a great help for the growing of vegetables but they could only be grown in the small space close up to the wall of a house. I grew a sweet corn crop seven feet high and carrots one foot long but these were planted under very favourable conditions in the vegetable garden of Arthur and Martha Rogers, which as well as being situated in a natural hollow several feet deep, was protected by a large New Zealand flax hedge.

To construct a large number of gardens of this nature would have taken months of labour and the few oxen available would soon be weakened by the carting of the necessary quantity of stones. Who could afford to experiment on work of this nature while in the meantime they would be neglecting their potato patches, their very life blood? They would have had to leave their fishing and the fetching of wood for later on and the feeling of almost sure frustration in the wake of imminent gales contributed to their decision that it 'ain't worth the while'.

We left the island after two years without giving them anything of real value in this direction, although one member of the meteorological station did succeed in getting more from his packet seeds, than we did. The details of his initial success went unrecorded but it was reported that after a while he gave it up as a bad job for some reason or other. How typically Tristan!

Christmas

One of the most important festivals of the year in the lives of the islanders of Tristan da Cunha was the festival of Christmas. The 2,000 year old story of the birth of Christ took the foremost place in the islanders mind on that day. I was fortunate enough to spend Christmas twice on Tristan da Cunha, the first time in 1937 when the island was still its old self and had been seldom visited by strangers and now as part of this invasion.

Having spent nearly two years on the island I was able to record a little about their Christmas activities when everyone gives themselves up to good feeling and merry-making.

As Christmas approached the women were the busiest people on the island. For months beforehand they treasured any new piece of cloth or print that they could lay their hands on, so that they would be able to have new dresses, new frocks and 'kappies', sun bonnets, for their children, who always came first in matters of this kind.

In the olden days, when there was no meteorological station on the island and hence no naval store or canteen, the menfolk used to go off to passing ships to barter suits for themselves and cloth for their women folk in exchange for fresh mutton, model boats, polished cow horns and other island souvenirs. But ships were scarce and they were lucky indeed if they saw a ship once a year. Print for the women's dresses was more difficult to obtain than suits for the men as ships' companies usually have a 100% male crew and it was only an occasional luxury liner or passenger vessel on a world cruise which presented the possibility of obtaining print for their new Christmas dresses. Often enough, therefore, the women had to be content with unpicking men's pyjamas and sewing them up into 'stripy' dresses and blouses and such women's wear was a common sight at the island. With the introduction of a Naval establishment at the island during the war, a little print was obtainable at the canteen.

From Christmas Eve, until the day after New Year's Day, the Tristans celebrated a holiday and only enough work is done during that period to carry them over into the New Year. Weeks before, however, the women concentrated on their new dresses while the men made running repairs about the house as well as attending to their fishing and farming.

Wood for burning had to be fetched from the mountain side and around the beaches by boat, and new moccasins had to be made for all. When the potato crops were flowering their patches had to be visited daily in the early mornings by gangs of people in order to kill the plague of 'grubs', caterpillars, which attacked the potato plants. A few days before Christmas was spring cleaning time and the houses were scrubbed out methodically room by room. Curtains were taken down and washed and in some houses a treasured table cloth was produced from an old sea chest and given its festive place of honour on the homemade table in the 'outside room', as their living room was called. Not every household was lucky enough to possess a room which was not a kitchen-cum-living room combined.

The next consideration, and naturally a most important one, was food for feasting and merry making. The day before Christmas Eve the boys took the dogs out along the plateau and rounded up every sheep on the island. They were driven home to the Settlement for selection and every man turned into a farmer, as though at the local village stock fair, making a careful choice of the sheep he would kill for his Christmas dinner. All the sheep were marked by identification splits and cuts in the ears and every man knew his own sheep by its markings.

Naturally, for such a festive occasion the best was always chosen and, after the slaughter, the men strolled from house to house to see who had the finest mutton with the thickest 'lard'. The conversation centred around mutton for the next day or two. The less industrious ones who had killed off their sheep on fine days instead of working at their potatoes, and hence producing greater crops, usually came in for their share of meat too, for on Tristan nearly everyone was related in some way to everyone else. The good islanders never let a single island family go without their Christmas dinner, no matter how lazy they might have normally been, as Christmas was a time of forgiving, thanksgiving and rejoicing, which they knew just as well as any other community in the world.

The women too were busy with food, in fact except for the actual killing they were, by far, busier than their men folk. For weeks and months ahead they saved flour, sugar, currants and anything else they could obtain, to bake cakes and puddings for their Christmas dinner. The great day arrived and meat was roasted in plenty of fat for, at this season, everyone could afford to be generous and this otherwise valuable commodity was not spared.

If there were already some new potatoes to be had, these were dug by the men, some were boiled and as many as would fit into the pot were roasted with the meat. The island children were up the side of the mountain with their old syrup and baking powder tins to pick a type of cranberry which grows wild and makes good eating. Berry pie was steamed for an additional pudding. Some may have managed to save a tin of canned fruit given from a passing ship which was certainly produced. Canned fruit was usually considered the height of luxury for the dining table in a land where nothing much more than a few apple trees will grow on account of the strong gales which strike the island every year.

Another commodity which was practically worth its weight in gold to the islanders was custard powder, and here again if one family was lucky enough to possess a tin, they certainly shared it with those not so fortunately situated. In return they might get some salt, or even baking powder, to make the potato pudding less heavy!

In the 'outside world' people often go away for Christmas, by train or car to some other town or village for our Christmas holiday. But there was no such escape for the Tristan islanders who have never seen such things as trains, motor cars or in fact anything on wheels apart from their old fashioned two-mile-an-hour home-made bullock carts. They did however 'go away' for Christmas by visiting their special friends for the whole period of the Christmas holiday. Arthur and Martha Rogers might arrange to spend Christmas with Johnnie and Sophia Green, in which case Arthur and Martha had all their meals, including breakfast, every day with Johnnie and Sophia, and only returned to their own home in the evenings to sleep.

The first thing Gordon Glass did on Christmas morning was to go down to the island flagstaff before anyone was up and to hoist the Union Flag, for this was one of the proudest little colonies. The flag was flown on special occasions such as Christmas, Easter day and upon such occasions as the arrival of a ship. Presently, the church bell was heard calling them and the cooks of the day will be the first into 'Arly Sarvice'.

Later, at possibly eight o'clock but at a time depending upon the missionary, was 'second service' for on such occasions the church is too small to hold everyone at once. The cooks by now were well on their way roasting the meat, making the berry pies and grating the potatoes for puddings. All who could possibly come made an effort to be present and the hymns and carols, so well known and beloved of the Church of England, were sung with gusto, albeit with a bit of a drawl.

The women were all dressed up in their new clothes with beads around their necks and handkerchiefs over their heads, for Tristan women never, under any circumstances, wore hats. Likewise, the children were in their best, with new 'kappies' of various colours on their heads. The menfolk donned their best suit, with collars, ties and even proper pairs of shoes or boots to replace the otherwise common moccasin.

In their lapels they wore button holes, marigolds or daisies and those who had medals, badges or brooches of any description proudly pinned them on for the great day. The last thing they did on Christmas Day was to put on their watches, which were seldom worn, in order that they were not out of commission on such important occasions.

They filed into church, which was packed up to the very last seat. Children sat right up at the front, even on the dais steps, with the women in the centre and the men all together right at the back. The altar was decorated with flowers from their gardens, and the Church was spotlessly clean having been scrubbed out from back to front the day before. The ordinary Church of England Christmas Matins, albeit in these slightly unusual surroundings, proceeded. Babies in arms howled from time to time and the missionary could not be heard. Sometimes passing the child on to other girls to be nursed quietened them, otherwise the mothers took them outside into the fresh air as this was usually the only cure.

After the service the women rushed home to get on with the cooking. The men, accompanied by the children, sauntered from house to house leaning on the gates or garden wall smoking their cigarettes or drawing on their pipes if they were lucky enough to have any tobacco. They talked of ships which had called in the past, of visitors such as the Norwegian Scientific Expedition, and also our invasion. Many remembered the various missionaries and their wives who spent periods of anything from three to six years on the island in the past and who had done such valuable work in educating the children to the best of their ability.

During my first Christmas on Tristan da Cunha the islanders, with their well known hospitality towards strangers, showered the thirteen scientists with presents of mutton, eggs, milk and even new potatoes and each of the forty-two families came down to our Expedition Headquarters to wish us the compliments of the season.

Our naval influx of some twenty strangers presented a very great difficulty to them with their very limited resources, for they likewise wished to treat them in the same way that they had treated the Norwegians. Fortunately, however, islanders and sailors had formed into cliques and there was no general distribution from the islanders in the way of presents at the Naval Station. Some islanders, however invited sailors up to their homes for dinner and many were presented with home-knitted socks, pullovers and scarves.

I was one of these fortunate ones and spent Christmas 1942 with Arthur and Martha Rogers at their home. 'Going away' for Christmas also as their guests were Victor and Lily Rogers and their daughter Joan. Joanie, a sweet little girl full of character, aged two and a half years of age, was called after my sister in England whom she had never seen and I always regarded her as one of my godchildren although she in reality was not. I made Joanie hang up a Christmas stocking and after a large dinner decorated a piece of island tree with a Union flag and real Christmas decorations, which Martha had possessed and treasured for years, received from an overseas friend from afar, not knowing exactly what they were meant for!

We broke the usual island custom, no presents at Christmas, and presented gifts to one another. It was indeed strange that birthdays were the only occasions on the island when presents were handed round. The giving of presents, the hanging of stockings and the Christmas tree were things quite alien to the Tristan mind, probably due to the general scarcity of everything at the island. But the true meaning of Christmas, with the birth of Christ and the story of Joseph and Mary were never far from their thoughts on this important day.

In 1942 some kind strangers from the 'outside world', such as Dr and Mrs Woolley, Padre Lawrence and Mr Reg Stoyel, gave large parties for the children down at the Naval Station and what with tea, cakes, sweets, bread and butter and jam, these children of isolation had the happiest time of their lives. Some of us even entertained the grown-ups to tea parties and dinners. On Boxing Day they liked to have a football match and in the evening they had a dance to which all but the children were invited. Again everyone was in his Sunday best, and those young men who possessed a pair of white tennis flannels produced them in which to dance their flat-footed island 'steps', waltzes and fox-trots, all of them far from anything we know by those names. Their orchestra consisted of a concertina and possibly an old violin, but these were usually played separately.

Perhaps some of us in the 'outside world' more fortunately situated will think once or twice of these men, women and children on this lonely island, who knew no Christmas trees or stockings, no great exchange of presents and no real holiday with a change of atmosphere. There were no shops and hotels, cinemas, fun fairs or even intoxicating liquors, things that we in the 'outside world' all take as a matter of course. But the Tristan people were happy and contented with what little they had and when they went to bed on Christmas Day I knew that, in their traditional simplicity, they knelt at their bedsides full of praise and thankfulness for their comparatively lucky lot.

Law and Order

"Yes, Sar," said Chief, "I 'speck the people will soon get used to it, but I's sure it will be a bit strange at first."

Incredible though it may seem, but these words were spoken by a man of forty, who had never used money of any description in the whole of his life. They were the words of Willie Repetto, Chief Islander of Tristan da Cunha, spoken at a Council meeting of islanders on 2 December 1942 when Dr Woolley, as Magistrate of the island, had asked the Tristan islanders whether they favoured the introduction of money for the first time in their history!

Up to that time they had always got along quite well without any currency and all trade was carried out by a system of bartering. The islanders were not all fools and knew well the value of a barrel of flour in relation to a sheep with the Head Islander arranging the exchange for the good of the islanders as a whole. This community of souls, living in the middle of the South Atlantic had managed to live in comparative contentment and happiness without any written laws of any description for well over one hundred years.

With the community well-established in the 1830s it might have seemed advisable to introduce some sort of government but apart from general consent and acknowledgement of Corporal William Glass as being the Head man, nothing was attempted. Upon his death in 1853, Pieter Groen, a Dutch castaway from a schooner wrecked in 1836, succeeded Glass and after his death in 1902, the island was without a representative of the community until the day Father Partridge asked them to elect a Headman in conjunction with the instigation of his Council.

Some twelve years previously, in 1930, the Revd Partridge, the Church of England minister on the island, realised that the islanders were tending to drift into a 'don't care happy-go-lucky' way of life. He decided to create a small council of islanders who could be called together to discuss certain matters of interest and value to the island as a whole. Such things, such as the dividing out of foodstuffs obtained from passing ships and the advisability of building up a piece of road that had got washed away in a recent heavy downpour, were subjects for discussion by a representative body of the best class of islanders, so Father Partridge as he was called, nominated about a dozen men and instituted the first Tristan Council.

These men were given certificates signed by him as Commissioner of the Island, a status conferred on him by the Colonial Office in London under whose jurisdiction the island came. These men were called together now and again which was a good thing for the island with its rich and poor, lazy and industrious, as an authority which they would be able to respect.

The example set by the Councillors, being the pick of the bunch of about one hundred and forty five, had a good influence on the islanders who otherwise might have let things slide too much in their independence.

Father Partridge left Tristan da Cunha in 1932 and the Council he instituted seldom met again except in a casual sort of way, such as in someone's house or outside in the village where several of them may have gathered together in a group.

It was in this state that we found the island when we arrived. Doctor Woolley decided that the Councillors should be reinstated. After making enquires and obtaining a list of the defunct Council, he nominated en block, ten of the most suitable men and me as I knew the islanders well. At a meeting of the whole island held in the Church, he put his proposal before the community and asked them if they would agree.

No one raised any objection and so the eleven men were presented with their certificates of membership in the presence of everyone.

It is strange but creditable that the islanders chose William Peter Repetto as their figurehead, for he was one of the quietest men on the island and one of the only bachelors in 1930. But Willie was a wise man preferring silence to unnecessary tittle tattle and his judgement was always sound and fair. He was the son of an Italian castaway who arrived at the island in the year 1892 and his mother Mrs Frances Repetto was one of the most respected women on the island.

It was a good thing for Tristan that many of the men who have come to the island either of their own accord or involuntarily have been deeply religious and God-loving men. From time to time the S.P.G. in London sent missionaries, and it is these men, together with the good people who have founded the island's unwritten laws based on sound common sense, the bible and the ten commandments.

The islanders behaved so well in the course of time that there was never any major crime of any description. One man who committed suicide was a settler from the 'outside world'. There have been no murders, no divorces and the islanders seemed a very tranquil type and not given to extremes of emotion in connection with their love affairs. On the contrary, although many were as well matched as any couple could be, terms of endearment such as we know were on the whole, but not exclusively, seldom used.

There was no written law at Tristan and no record of what happened when something did occur. Crime was so rare that there was practically nothing on record as to what happened to so and so when he stole the potatoes or did some other petty theft, nor what the islanders would have done in the case of crime and how punishment would have been meted out, in spite of the fact that the Tristan people were perfectly normal human beings.

In hard times a starving islander had been known to break into someone's potato shed at night and steal potatoes. All that was done in cases like that was ostracism. Everybody discussed the crime for the want of something better to talk about and the culprit was made to feel miserable. It is not organised in any way but more instinctive. The matter was reported to Chief, who may pass some remark next time he saw him, such as 'You all best leave them taties alone what belongs to other peoples'.

Naturally the boys on Tristan were as human as any others and had spasms of naughtiness. Petty thieving, as existing in any household in the world, happened at times, and what boy in the world will not raid the cupboard which holds the sugar, raisins and jam? Not that the islanders often possessed such luxuries but after the visit of a 'good' ship their larders were comparatively full.

Should there be anything like a murder on the island the Head Islander would wait for the next ship and report the matter to the Captain. The ship would probably be bound for the Cape and the matter in all probability would reach the Commander-in-Chief of the Royal Naval Station at Simonstown and he would probably send a man-o'-war to the island, at his convenience, to investigate. In the meantime the guilty islander would probably have led his normal life for there is no gaol on Tristan and in any case there was no escape to the nearest inhabited land, St. Helena.

There was no court house on the island, likewise no 'traffic cops' as their only transport was bullock carts and donkeys. There were no proper roads and, although called 'roads', the few tracks around the Settlement were really nothing more than cart tracks through the grassy plateau. I have no idea as to whether the 'rule of the road – keep left' would apply if two bullock carts met going down to the beach to bring up stores. They would probably instinctively have taken the course most suited whether left or right!

The islanders were very healthy and died usually either of old age or accidents. Infectious diseases were fortunately unknown but it was difficult to imagine what would happen if a passing ship introduced something like measles or mumps. They might prove to have extremely little internal resistance to such maladies and might well have died off quite quickly.

When deaths occurred on Tristan there were no courts of enquiry or inquests. Post mortems were unknown and the bodies were buried in one of the two small island cemeteries at the bottom of the Settlement. Coffins were made of driftwood or packing cases and the padre, or the head islander in his absence, holds the service. After a death the property went to the next of kin and islanders seldom made out wills, although this had been done in a simple way.

There was an island register, introduced somewhere around the 1870s. Births, Deaths and Marriages were recorded therein by missionary or headman, little else however appeared in the book and no birth certificates were issued.

When ships arrived at the island, the Captain sometimes called for a sheep which would be the object for barter for the community. Chief would then call for a volunteer to produce one and the islanders kept a note of who had contributed in the past. So they took 'each one they turn' as they said and in a lifetime an islander might well miss altogether. The poorest who had no sheep, or very few, would never be asked to contribute on such occasions.

Tristan was no place for a lawyer. The islanders fought their own battles and such things as defamation might well be dealt with by 'one under the lug' but I never heard of anything so serious as this happening. Lawyers were likewise not required to look after land or title deeds. All land was free to anyone who cared to build a wall round a selected spot so long as he kept that ground under cultivation otherwise it could be taken by anyone in need of fresh ground.

Before an islander married he selected a site for his house close to a stream at the Settlement. Out of respect, he would inform Chief of his choice who would probably raise no objection. Doubtless Chief would ask 'When you all going to build your house?' and the reply would possibly be 'after we's done spading' or 'after the boats get back from Nightingale'. This was an island thirty miles distant which they visit occasionally for sea birds and their eggs, as well as guano and petrel fat.

This was the basis of life on the isolated spot where they lived without laws, without crime and in general contentment and happiness. This was the life they were leading when we arrived at the island as a military detachment on 5 April 1942.

Council Meetings

After Doctor Woolley re-instituted the island council matters of interest, such as Station dogs chasing sheep, were discussed to the mutual advantage of all.

Our meetings were held down at the padre's quarters, and we would all be seated around a room on chairs with our backs to the wall, with the doctor and padre presiding at a table at one end of the room. The men would all congregate together in the Settlement and arrive in a body. After "Good evening, Sar" all round, they took their places and the doctor began with the business of the day.

The Island Council, 1943.

Back: Fred Swain, John Green, Ned Green

Middle: Joseph Repetto, Arthur Rogers, Thomas Glass, John Lavarello, Gordon Glass

Front: Henry Green, Willie Repetto (Chief Islander), Johnnie Repetto

The islanders were very shy at first and seldom did anything but agree with their characteristic "Yes Sar" and "No Sar". They had great respect for the chair.

First Meeting: 2 December 1942

In the evening at Padre's house, we were all present to discuss some vital problems. Dr Woolley opened proceedings.

"I have had a signal from Simonstown in the Cape approving payment of 1/- a day for work at the Naval Station helping the soldiers to build. But I have already put in a report suggesting 2/- is more suitable for the work done. At present the system of paper money 'chits' which we are using involves a tremendous amount of typing, followed by scissor-work to cut them into small pieces. Padre and I are in favour of a plan to introduce money to the island to save all this work and it may also be possible to introduce some sort of bank, with headquarters and trustees in the Cape, Mr Snell for instance whom you all know, in the absence of a padre and myself. You are closely connected to the Cape now that a meteorological station has been built on the island.

"The introduction of money might cause a bit of trouble at first because you would have to learn how many pennies there are in a shilling, how many shillings in a pound and, most importantly, what money is worth. We would have to hold lectures on money."

Here Henry Green, one of the oldest inhabitants, showed signs of restlessness and it was obvious that he had something to say. Dr Woolley gave him his cue.

"Sar! They used to have money in the olden days. The old hands used to get it off the whalers. But I guess it's h'all gorn now. I guess these is only the old hands what could understand it and I h'expect they's all done forget about it now. They used to get £1 I think it was for a sheep and beef sold for 4d a pound. The whalers used to go for potatoes and the Americans used to give one dollar for a bushel of taters."

Old Henry's knowledge astounded everyone, but none of those present except him had seen those days and had no idea of the true value of the money.

"I think it would be a good idea and it would be less work for the doctor on them papers," said Chief as he sprang into life.

"It would make things much easier for me, Willie."

"Yes Sar, I'se sure it would."

Doctor asked me what I thought about it.

"I think it would be a good idea too and I suggest it might be possible to make South African and English money interchangeable. After all the coins are the same size and every ship that comes to the Island has either been to Cape Town or is bound there."

"We shall have to see about that," said the doctor, "There might be complications of exchange, but I don't think so. The South African pound and the English are almost the same value. Anyway do you all agree to the introduction of money?"

"It would be alright," said Johnnie Repetto, who has never bought or sold a thing for cash in his life.

"It might be a bit awkward at first," put in his brother, Joe.

"It would be a good idea," Fred Swain followed.

"I take it you are all agreed?"

"Yes, Sar," came a chorus from the islanders.

"Well now we can get along with the next thing," continued the doctor, " Some of you have quite a lot of money to your credit in my book – one or two have got over £15. When people in the 'outside world' save money they put it in what is called a bank. They lend the money and the bank uses it and makes it more. The money is safe for you to use whenever you like, and at the same time you are getting paid for putting it there. One pound in a bank can become one pound and six pence after a year if you don't spend it".

Doctor then asked if there were any questions. All the islanders looked lost and there was no reply. After a pause he asked if they understood the bank.

"Money can be drawn out any time."

"Yes, Sar," sang the chorus.

"Padre and I would look after it for you, we would run your bank so long as we are here and when we leave the money can be paid back to the owners or transferred to Mr. Snell in the Cape who would look after it for you. People could write to him for things they needed. Do you all understand?"

"Yes, Sar," came the chorus.

"That would be a good idea," commented the Chief.

"That would be the best idea," added Henry.

"Good. Now, about the extra shilling. Up till now you have been getting a shilling a day but it is going to be made into two shillings. That's to say all islanders will have another shilling coming for each one they have earned. That means there is quite a lot of money to come. It works out at about £15 in one week for the whole island. Don't forget, now that the construction work is coming to a close there will be no work left – or very little – and now is the chance to save. You will have to

A money token, numbered with its value.

think about the winter coming too, when some will need more than others," and the Doctor offered cigarettes all round.

"You see, Chief, with a bank each man has a book which he keeps with him with his money written down. Is that all clear? You had better ask the other islanders what they think about it".

"Yes, Sar," repeated the chorus.

"Now the next item is wood. We have got a nice pile of wood left over from the construction and I am sure some of the islanders would like the chance to buy some to board out their houses. Some houses have only stone walls and that makes them damp and bad for you in the winter. We shall have to keep some pieces for repair and extensions."

"Yes, Sar, sure you will," butted in Chief.

"Some of the wood can be paid to the islanders as a whole for general services rendered and I suggest it be used for the new Parish Hall. We shall have to see how much wood is wanted and how much we must keep. Then we could have a sale. Captain Sayers left a list of the prices of all the various types of wood and I assure you the prices are very high but as much is damaged I think I can take the line that it isn't as good as when it was landed," to which there was general laughter.

"I suggest reducing the price to the islanders to a half. Here is the list. That is to say 3 inches by 4½ inches costs 1/- per foot, (laughter) I suggest selling for sixpence. 3 by 3 is 8d a foot, and I suggest 4d. 1½ by 4½ is strong and suitable for floor boarding – that is 6d, and I suggest 3d. Ceiling boarding can go at 1½d a foot – it cost the government 3d. – and weather boarding can go at half price of two feet for a penny farthing. One day's pay of two shillings is now worth 4/- a day when it comes to wood."

Doctor then explained how the government bought stores in bulk and we got it from the government to build at cost price.

"When we pay 2/- for wood, others pay 3/-, and so on. So you see we do well that way and the wood is all new. There will be quite a pile of odds and ends which Willie can divide out. It is not on the books, it will be a gift. Is that all clear?"

"Yes, Sar, yes," came the chorus again.

The doctor asked padre to say what he had to say about the building of the new Parish Hall.

"I have discussed the new Parish Hall with Captain Sayers when he was on the island and he made recommendations here and there, which we shall be able to put into effect. The new hall should be sixteen feet wide. The easiest thing would be to rebuild. Blue stone walls I am afraid will be too damp. We shall build it out of soft stone. It will be sixty feet long and the doctor says we can have some corrugated iron which is left over for the roof. Is there plenty of soft stone, Chief?"

"There's plenty, Sar," said Chief, "but only a few pieces came down when the soldiers blast. It's dangerous work up there on the side of the hill. If you slip you's gorn!"

"When the gangs get finished at the station we shall put them on building the new hall," continued padre, but Chief looked glum.

"Father, don't see how we can do it. The men have got all of their island work to do and if the grubs come they won't get a tater. Grubs stripped a patch in one day last year down Old Pieces. The grubs is starting now and they go on before and after Christmas. Every morning the island men is up before breakfast as regular as clockwork."

Little notice was taken of this explanation and padre asked when they could start.

"Perhaps the end of February! Got to keep going all the time." Henry Green suggests, who amongst all the other islanders is not a bit keen on starting the work at this time of the year.

"Is a new Parish Hall wanted?" Doctor enquired, somewhat annoyed.

"Yes, Sar, the men is willing. But how can they do it with five pair of bullocks? That's all the bullocks the men got left on the island now," Chief replied.

"Chief, do you know what chance you are throwing away?" Padre added impatiently.

"Yes, Sar, I ain't throwing away any chances but how can the men do it? When they built the church they had twenty pair of bullocks. They're only five now and they're young bullocks, not like them old ones."

Here doctor offered the use or the Station tractor. And the offer was appreciated although the men were still solid in their opinion that now was not the time, just as the potatoes were ripening and I firmly adhered to their views.

"Next item is Pigs. What about those pigs being taken over to Inaccessible? When can you do it, Chief?"

"First day we get, Sar. First day I sees a good day I'm going to take them over myself."

"I nearly shot a pig the other day. If they get into the garden Big Gordon and I are going to build they will be shot," the Doctor said.

There was a round of laughter from everyone.

There was an interval at this stage and everyone lit up a cigarette. Padre went out into his kitchen and a few minutes afterwards appeared with a tray of cups of tea. Over tea they discussed informally the introduction of money and agreed that they would soon "larn" how to use it. The conversation reverted to grubs as they finished tea and the meeting continued in earnest. There was a much better atmosphere after tea but the grubs were still foremost in everyone's mind.

"You can clear away every grub in one day until there is not a grub left. Then next day there'll be millions. I don't care, Sar, I'd rather do the hardest day's work than go grubbing. Johnnie and Arthur went out one day and they were so thick with grubs the potato plants was bending over. They couldn't hold the weight. Reverend Wilde tried to spray them and killed the taters!" Joe Repetto said.

"I picked for so long one time," put in Johnnie Repetto, "that my back ached."

"What are these grubs like, Willie? Could you bring me a sample in a matchbox some day when you are going out?"

"Yes, Sar. If it wasn't for the grubs some years you'd get so many taters I guess you wouldn't know what for to do with them. They'd be too many to h'eat," Chief replied.

"When I was a boy I never knew what a grub was. We used kelp in those days to manure a patch. If you use kelp you don't get half as many grubs," Henry added.

"Well I think this grub business has been dealt with. Has anyone any more business?" the Doctor continued.

"Yes, Sar. What about them geese? There's no ships and the islanders won't know what to do with them," Chief commented.

There were recent rumours on the island that there were far too many geese eating the grass the cattle should be eating, with the result that they were dying in the bad weather through shortage of grass.

"Well I don't know whether you have ever heard of Pitcairn. It is a small island in the Pacific with also a small community. The island was over-run with goats and the men got together and decided that they kill off all their goats except for three to each family. There was a plague of goats then, we have a plague of geese!", to which there was much laughter at the Doctor's story.

"Now what about Anchorstock sheep? They are without a ram and the ram is with the home sheep."

"I reckon their ram is stopping out the Molly Gulch and he won't budge," put in Johnnie the Baptist and doctor suggested a couple of boys should carry it round the Bluff back to Anchorstock.

"I guess it will take a couple of men! Boys can't handle it. What they want to do is to put a rope round its neck and lead it. You'd have to hold the rope short or it might fall off. If no one will take it I'll take it myself - me an' Fred an' Thomas," Chief suggested.

"Don't let Chief and Fred an' Thomas take it! They'll h'eat him up before they get him over there," there were roars of laughter from everyone at Henry's comment.

"Now what about the wool? The wool must be ready for shearing and it is good wool," continued the doctor.

"I suggest, Sar, they divide it out into small lots. Otherwise they will only get a handful each and it wouldn't be worth it," Chief said.

"I believe the Station sheep have got ticks," added the doctor.

"Yes Sar. The sheep what come have got ticks but there's none on the h'island sheep. I didn't know what they was when I sees them. We's never seen them on the h'island before," the Chief informed them.

"If they ever had any they must have died out. Well, if there isn't any more business I think we will close and go home. Good night everybody." as the doctor concluded proceedings.

"Goodnight, Sar!" chorused the men as they picked up their hats to go.

After the meeting padre button-holed Chief and asked him to stay behind. He also asked me to remain as he wanted to discuss something. Then when every one was gone he exploded.

"Look here, Willie, there's been enough things given away on this island without a thank you. Do you realise the doctor gave you all that wood, enough to build a new Parish Hall and there wasn't so much as a thank you from all those men".

"Father, how can we build a hall? Any other year this time we's done make our manure and is started grubbing. Now with all the work the men's had helping the soldiers build the station for the last eight month they ain't done a thing. Our people will starve."

"Every time anybody tries to help you, you put up difficulties in the way every time," the padre interjected.

"I ain't putting no difficulties in the way, Father."

"All right, Chief. Good night."

"Good night, Sar," said Chief as he and I departed for the Settlement.

On the way up he explained all over again to me how the men have got to think of their families at this time of the year, otherwise 'the grubs will get a hold to they taties and you's going to have none for to put in your bins when digging time come round'.

I had not spoken a word throughout the arguments at the meeting nor afterwards. I made it known to the doctor and padre that I was sympathetic with the islanders' views. As regards the absence of 'thank you' the men were far too occupied with their opinion of the inadvisability of building the Hall at the present time to accept the offer with enthusiasm. Under normal circumstances I knew the islanders well enough and they were always grateful for any gifts but their minds were too pre-occupied. Knowing the islanders minds and mentality as well as I did I knew that they were very shy and did not wish to be too grasping when doctor made his offer.

No other meetings of the island Council were needed for three months, and during that time many things came to a head and doctor felt it necessary to call them together again.

Second Meeting: 3 March, 1943

Word went round that a meeting would be held down at the Padre's at eight o'clock. All eleven councillors were present, with doctor and padre as before in the chair. Doctor got down to business without any to do.

"Now I have a list here, and the first item on the agenda is in connection with school. I propose school should be held from Mondays to Fridays. There would have to be three different classes. The Parish Hall is not suitable, it is too small. I suggest we use three rooms in some of the houses close to the Church."

The Councillors agreed that between Harry Swain, Johnnie Repetto, Fred and Tom Rogers all of whom had 'outside rooms' they said that it would easily be arranged.

"All right, Chief, will you please handle the matter and let me know which rooms you are going to use. Of course, I don't deny that there will be a certain amount of inconvenience caused and children are bound to make a mess, but the mess can be cleared up by the mothers and big sisters."

The next item on the agenda was a discussion in connection with Air Raid Precautions.

"If a German ship were to arrive at the island and start throwing shells, everyone would rush round in mad circles. Padre has got a scheme and we must have a meeting of the whole island to discuss the matter and tell them what to do. A day is wanted. Most people have now finished digging and they will soon all be home. I think the best alarm to sound if a ship unexpectedly appears would be the church bell. How about Monday, at say 3 p.m.?"

"I expect I shall be on the Peak" I told doctor.

"Well, how about Tuesday? Will you be down by then?"

I said I would.

"All right then, if everybody is agreeable we'll have it near the church at 3 p.m., or I think 2.30 would be better. Will you tell everyone on the island, Chief, 2.30 on Tuesday afternoon, beside the Church?"

Chief said he would, and doctor then proceeded with item three.

"Now about lavatories. The present position is a shocking bucket-type and flies breed. A day may come when someone may land with a germ which the flies carry and you'll all die. I am going to suggest that everybody, every family on the island, has a deep-pit type lavatory and I am going to make it compulsory.

"We have plenty of old forty-four gallon drums left over at the station and I am going to give two to each family. The drums will be sunk in the ground, one on top of the other, with a box over them to form a seat. Each one must have a lid which must always be kept shut when not in use, to prevent the flies getting in and laying their eggs. The danger of flies has now been minimised by the introduction of pipe lines laid by the soldiers. Previously ducks, geese, sheep, pigs, dogs and cattle all drank and wallowed in the island's water supply and then they carry the germs. They get the germs from dung, tread in the water and then you drink it! Someday something very serious might happen if nothing is done to rectify that very serious matter. Anyway, I'll talk to the island as a whole and in the meanwhile Chief, your men can talk to the islanders about the dangers of flies and the construction of the new lavatories. The best way to get them done properly is to get the work gangs to do them, starting from the west and working to the east doing each house in turn until the job is finished. I'm going to put Marlow in charge of this work to see that it is done properly.

"Next item, geese. In future each family on the first of May each year must not possess more than three geese. It doesn't matter how many geese they sit each year so long as by 1 May they have only three left. You have got two months now in which to dispose of your geese and if ships come I suggest you try to trade as many as you can. Some of you will have to have roast goose for dinner every Sunday for the next few weeks! (*laughter*) On 1 May everyone must block up their geese in their potato sheds or somewhere, and the Councillors will go round from house to house and count them to see that nobody has more than three. Then there will be, let me see, fifty families make 150 geese instead of 1500 (*much laughter*) but I don't think there are anything like that number on the island." It was the doctor's joke which was much appreciated.

"Now about 'sailo'. There have been far too many false alarms about ships lately. I know the culprits mean nothing wrong, but in these days we have to be prepared and if a false alarm is given, that a ship is in sight it puts us to a lot of unnecessary trouble. Islanders must stop singing 'She'll be coming round the mountain when she comes', even as a joke, because it gives rise to the belief that there is a ship in sight."

There was much uproarious laughter all round. The islanders had learnt that popular tune from the soldiers who were always singing it. It fitted well because most ships, at any rate all ships from the Cape, do actually 'come round the mountain when they come'.

"I am going to offer a prize, which will hold all the time I am on the island, of three packets of twenty cigarettes to the man that reports first to me when a ship really is in sight. If they try pulling one another's leg, they won't believe it when a ship really does come and then it will be too late."

"Sure it would, Sar," replied Chief.

The shouting on the sighting of a ship off the island was a relic of the days of sail and there was great excitement when the first person shouted 'sailo'.

"Now, there is a very Serious matter which has to be dealt with. It has come to my ears that the children have started swearing. They learnt it from the soldiers. Now, if I hear any child swear, I shall give it a 'hammering' myself. If anyone hears any children swear, the fathers must give them one too. Councillors must 'hammer' children they hear swearing."

"Now, about the spare rifles there are on the island. We have just over a dozen and the islanders should use these against Japs and Germans which may try to land at the island at any time. I am sure the men would like to have a whack at them," to which there were subdued cries of 'sure', "and I am going to ask Chief to make a list of a dozen or so keen men who are good shots with a rifle. I am going to ask Mr. Crawford to look after this home guard and you could have target shooting practices and manoeuvres on the Plateau. Twelve men with rifles would make it difficult for an enemy to land if the machine gun posts were overwhelmed. If they succeeded in getting into the Settlement they might do what they like with the island women and children. I should get together some married men and some single, Chief, and arrange them into two lots, eastward and westward for convenience. At present the Bluff is undefended."

"They would not get past a small gang of our men out there, for we knows the road" reckoned John the Baptist.

"They would probably arrive about daylight. Now is that all clear? Any questions?"

There were none.

Will you look after that for me?" enquired of me and I assured doctor that I would.

"I have had no word," said doctor, continuing the business of the day, "from the outside world with regard to the introduction of money on the island. If I don't hear before winter I shall make a signal for approval of pay by the chit system which we have been using. But in the meantime it would be better if I kept the money as some will only go and spend it and they won't have any when hard times come along. There is quite a lot of money owing!"

"There are so many sheep on the plateau I was wondering if we could put some up on the base. There is plenty of grass up there and it looks good to me."

"The hardest job would be carrying them up there," Henry said, "and when they's up there I 'spect they soon be down again . It's too thick snow up there winter time and they wouldn't like that."

Doctor and padre both talked about the successful breeding of sheep under these conditions in the Falkland Islands, Patagonia and Scotland where there is not much grass but mostly heather.

"Put them up near the Knobs, where Mr Crawford and them had they camp when the Norwegians was here, there's plenty of grass up there. I'd rather get rid of sheep than, loose cattle h'any day. I guess it is something like 200 lambs born h'every year. Me an' Arfer (Arthur) is going to have a try anyway. Once they are up there I guess they'll stop up there," Chief suggested.

Johnnie and Thomas agreed to try by themselves.

"Me and Fred is also going to have a try," said someone.

"I'm going to have a try on my own," added Joe Repetto in a burst of independence.

"I suggest," volunteered padre, "we put the lambs up there when they are old enough. Twenty sheep would make all the manure for one family that you are likely to need at the Settlement. Sheep eat up a lot of grass. Doctor wouldn't believe grass would grow on Tristan until they were blocked out the Molly Gulch. The other day I lost a wheel barrow in the fenced off part at the Station!

There was much laughter.

"Dog shooting has started!" the doctor interrupted.

There were peals of laughter all round. There had been trouble about dogs out at night which, being under-fed, sometimes chased sheep and ate the lambs, Only one dog was seen out last night, Cyril's. It was caught on a wire down at the old army camp and couldn't get away.

"It only take one bitch on heat for to see how many dogs are loose at night," Chief pointed out.

"Ther'r only two bitches on the h'island, and if it was more I don't know what it would be like."

"What about sister's dorg!" said a voice from the side referring to the Royal

Naval Nursing Sister's dog.

Again there was much laughter.

By 9.30 p.m. doctor and everyone was feeling tired and started to wind up proceedings.

"Do you all agree then to save money for the winter?"

"Well, I for my part agree", said Chief.

"Yes Sar", came the chorus.

"There is a shilling outstanding for each shilling earned, which means £600 has been paid out up to date. That means there is about £500 to come," the doctor informed them.

With 'Goodnight, Sar' all round the men left for their houses to discuss in some cases up till midnight with their wives and families all that had transpired.

Third Meeting: 2 June, 1943

Although there were no fixed days for the meetings of the Tristan da Cunha Councillors it so happened that on 2nd June, almost three months again to the day, doctor called his advisors together again for the third time. Every one was present, including the padre and myself, and the first item for discussion was lavatories.

Most of the work of construction and alteration had been completed at the Naval Station and doctor saw a chance to go ahead with the building of the lavatories.

With a black board and chalk he drew the type of things which had to be constructed and the Councillors took an intelligent interest in all he showed them.

"The gangs will be divided into two. Half will be employed on government work and the rest on this work," said doctor.

"Every islander will have to decide for himself where his lavatory will be situated. I can recommend on the east side of every house as the prevailing winds are westerly. I think we can start on Monday and at four o'clock in the afternoon on Friday I shall have a meeting of all the island men to explain the necessity for proper sanitation and the dangers of flies."

"Now padre informs me that the school furniture is nearly finished". Some of the better carpenters amongst the islanders had been helping him to make forms, benches and desks and a very fine show they put up too with padre as a good all round factotum at their head.

"You are not too pushed for work at present, that is so isn't it, Chief?"

"Yes, Sar, but spading has started but it isn't so much yet."

"Anyway, we shall start school in about a fortnight's time. Apart from the youngsters, boys between the ages of fourteen and eighteen have got to be pulled in too. School will be compulsory. Everybody has got to go. Everyone in the world, you Johnnie and you Gordon and even me, has got to do certain things and so have the children. They have got to go to school unless they are sick of course when they won't be able.

"Classes will be held from 5.30 to 7.30 every afternoon in the week. The men will come on Mondays and Tuesdays – the women on Thursdays and Fridays. Children's school will be from 2 o'clock to 4.30 in the afternoons of Mondays and Tuesdays, Thursdays and Fridays.

"A school house-cum-Parish Hall has got to be built," the Doctor was taking a firm line now, "and Padre has the plans. As soon as the lavatory business is finished, work must proceed. We shall want from five to ten men a day. The present Parish Hall is not big enough and the back wall has sunk. Wood is available for the job and it must be built to last. I am quite pleased with the work on the huts out at the patches. I suppose Chief will be thinking about building a wall out at the Bluff?"

"Yes, Sar."

"There will be time for that. It must be a good wall, a permanent one that the sheep will not be able to jump."

During the past week padre had been making improvements at the Church by running an electric light line on gum poles so that the services did not always have to be held in the daytime.

"Stays are needed for the electric light poles up to the Church otherwise a gale might come along and blow them all down. I think Friday would be a good day. There are twenty-six poles to be stayed, twenty-six poles to have the wires untied and twenty-six poles to be tied up again."

There was much laughter at the way padre expressed himself , especially so that there should be no misunderstanding.

"I for my part believe that they will all want back-stays, one to the h'east and one to the west," said Chief.

I suggested that the stays and the poles should be painted white because if someone shouted 'sailo!' they might run to the beach so fast that they would trip over the stays!

"Well, the next item on the agenda is a ship. I have just received a signal from the Cape that we are to expect a ship called the *British Power* in three days time. I believe there is one ton of tea aboard (*we had been short of tea for many months*). One ton of meal and lots of other stuff to unload. As long as is a good day we should get on quite fast. The men have had plenty of experience in that kind of work by now. Two hundred tons were off-loaded in a day off the *Cilicia*, and there were loads up to 600lbs. on the last ship. This time there is nothing more than 100lbs." The doctor paused.

"Doctor, will you please talk to the men about the dogs. The ewes are starting to lamb. Reginald and Sidney's dorg h'eat one of my lambs alive on the beach the other day. I'se done tell Sidney about it but what can you do?" the Chief interjected.

"If there is so much as a whisper that any dog is troubling the sheep they must be shot."

Chief was very agitated about the behaviour of the dogs and especially the Station dogs which belonged to the Naval ratings and meteorologists. He told his story of the lamb on the beach three times after which every one was fully conversant with the facts of the case.

"Reg Stoyell's dog and that Terry of the petty officer was after sheep on Sunday."

"That petty officer's dog has only got to twig a sheep and he's off!" added Johnnie Green.

Then followed various accounts from many of the Councillors of dogs they had seen chasing sheep.

"Will you be going ratting soon, Chief?" asked the padre, being reminded that dogs were used to seek out rats.

"Yes, Sar, when we can find a day. About the middle of the month, I reckon. Sometime after the ship. Would the doctor please give a day?"

"Right, Willie, I shall let you know when it would be suitable. How many rats do you catch in a day?"

"Over three hundred I reckon. Revd Wilde cut off their tails for to count them! Each one had a pot in his pocket in which he put his tails". Much laughter.

"They will get at least four hundred this time. What they want to do is to split up into gangs of 10 and part off, one would go this way and one would go that," said Johnnie Repetto with a typical biblical influence which the islanders often used.

"I am prepared to offer a prize of a packet of twenty cigarettes to each of the ten men in the gang that kills the largest number of rats. But there must be no cheating and they must bring back the tails in a tin to be counted," the doctor said amid laughter.

"Fred is as good as a dorg!" Johnnie Green joked to peals of laughter.

"His dorg allus hunt woodlice," someone else added to renewed laughter.

"John the Baptist got the best dorg," said Fred, deciding it was his turn to say something.

"Some dorgs allus lie. They say they's got a rats nest and you pull down the wall and there is nothing there," Johnnie Repetto mused.

Doctor suggested the sailors formed a gang and went too.

"Station dorgs might get too many sheep," observed Joe Repetto wryly.

After everyone had 'done' laughing as the islanders say, the meeting closed and every one went to their respective houses.

Things were beginning to look serious around July and August. Lazy islanders had eaten up nearly all their potatoes and the new crops would not be ready until January, in five months time. During this period these people had to live on fish and any work for other islanders in exchange for their food. But this was not a fair proposition because it meant that the lazy men get good meals occasionally whereas their wives and children got next to nothing. These men went off fishing and at the end of the day sent some little girl or boy with fish on a plate for this islander and that.

"It is the same old story that has been going on for fifty years at any rate, to my knowing," said old Mrs. Repetto one day over a cup of tea in her kitchen, "They sends the fish round with the children because they's too frightened for to go themselves. You see, in exchange for the fish Martha gives them potatoes and they know it before they go otherwise you can be sure them fellers wouldn't send their fish around. Mr. Crawford it's the old, old island story and we know all about it, just the same as you do, you's been on the island long enough now. Them's the fellers what spoil the Island and them's the fellers that give Tristan a bad name."

Fourth Council Meeting: 16 August, 1943

With ten or twenty children on starvation diets Doctor Woolley called his Councillors together for the fourth time.

"Last Saturday," he started "I spoke to all those who were short of potatoes. I ordered them to put in more ground and I told each one how many more he needed. I am not going to have children starving while I am on the island. The men have gone off already to do their work and when they are finished they must report to me. I shall tell certain Councillors to go out and examine their patches to see if they have done them properly

"There were some 525 patches and each man owned as many as he needed to feed his family throughout the year, or more correctly, should have done, which was the whole problem before us at the meeting.

"The trouble will be," Doctor went on to say, "that these people have even eaten up their seed! But they have got money and will be able to buy. Are there any people who have seed for sale? Are there any here?"

"Couldn't 'zactly say, Sar. I dare say I could spare few big taters, but there is obviously no great surplus this year therefore they will have to buy the potatoes and green them off to make seed," replied Chief.

"Children will need feeding soon, the same as last year, and they will have to pay for it too. There are possibly more children this time. The children are sent round asking for potatoes and this is bad. It is begging and that is bad. Then they take them home and the father has a good meal and the children get none. So this feeding has got to be done and there will probably be about 15 to 20 children who have to be fed. Now with regard to patches. Some men have had to put in new ground as I explained but I learnt while out there that the law doesn't make sense. To own ground you put up a wall anywhere you like and then it is yours. Is that right, Chief?"

"Yes, Sar. And after seven years a patch unspaded can be taken by anyone who fancies it".

"What can happen as things stand at present," Doctor went on, "is that anyone can fence in a patch and then do nothing. It is all wrong. A rogue could take the whole island by staking! I suggest a time limit. When a man wants more ground he can build a fence and if he hasn't worked that ground within six months he loses all claim to that plot for a year. Is that quite clear and do you agree? Don't forget, it must be completely fenced in."

"Yes, Sar," replied the chorus.

"When a man stakes a new patch he must tell Chief and he has lost it if there is no wall after six months. The reason for the year is that he could keep putting up the stones every six months and get away with it. If a man takes down a wall because he wants the stone, that land becomes common property. Even if he has only taken down one wall he has lost the right to that patch. That's right, isn't it Chief?"

"Yes, Sar."

"The next thing is the new Parish Hall. This will be done in the same way as the lavatories, one day a week, in gangs. This must be built. It will be similar to income and other taxes in the 'outside world'. You see we have to pay taxes and things and the Government builds halls and places which are useful to us. So the work you do you get back in another form. What have you got to say, Padre?"

"I think we should start on Wednesday so that we can get some thing done before the boats go over to Nightingale. It will be eight feet high, eighty feet long and consist of four rooms with partitions which can be taken down for dances. In one end will be a small store for books and school desks. We have got to supply our own materials. The old mission house on Little Beach Point is falling into disrepair but the stone is still good. We shall use that and pull it down altogether. There is still some good wood which can be used. The best place for the new Hall would be just behind the present one. There will be weather boarding on three sides and a small veranda in front. The roof will be of corrugated iron. The back wall must be away from the soil otherwise it gets damp. Digging will start on Wednesday. The mould (*islanders' word for soil*) we take out will be piled up on the east and west gable ends to act as a wind brake. The gangs should stay the same, as they are now, split into two."

"I reckon each gang what is split up should have a head man appointed by the head of the gang," Thomas Glass suggested.

Johnnie Repetto appointed Joe Repetto. John the Baptist appointed Gordon. Chief said he reckoned he will have to split up the gangs a bit more because his 'other half gang can't build a wall' to which there was laughter.

"They's built lavatory walls and they fall down. They's done fall down," he said, to more laughter. Chief thereupon appointed Fred to head of this gang.

"But I can't have all of them, they's too stupid," Fred said in an effort to get a better team which he succeeded in doing as Chief promised to let him have some good ones too.

Then followed a discussion about transport for the building of the new Parish Hall. Doctor asked them how they were going to come out on bullocks.

"Yes, Sar, bullocks is the problem. T'ain't many bullocks on the island an' September is the weakest month," Chief informed him.

"The end of October or the beginning of November they ought to be alright," Johnnie Green thought.

It turned out, after a discussion, that there were not more than twelve pairs of bullocks on the island. Padre suggested the stone be drawn all in one day and those without bullocks lend their carts. Doctor made a list of bullocks and carts while they all gave him the information.

"Henry got a cart," says some jocular sportsman, which produced subdued laughter.

"What?" replies Henry, "Guess I'se got to make a wheel first!"

There was much laughter. There was some special joke in connection with Henry's cart which we did not twig. I think he had been trying to repair it for some months and was frustrated each time for one reason or another.

"My pole's broke," says Joe Repetto.

"My cart's arm is broke," follows his brother Johnnie.

"My cart's arm is broke also," said Fred.

"Those who use bullocks and carts share out what timber is left over and we don't want after we have pulled down the old Mission House," Padre offered, hoping to give some inducement and kindle some enthusiasm. With twenty-one carts on the island and twenty bullocks it meant that only ten carts could be worked as bullocks were yoked in pairs.

"Ten carts will draw all the stone you want in two days," calculated Thomas.

"How about the tractor? I think we can spare it for the job. It will carry as much load as four carts. You could make a dump of stone alongside the road down at Little Beach Point and the tractor could bring it all up from there. The carts would work between the pile and the new site," the doctor countered.

"Thank you," said Padre, "I think we should get the job done now. The woodwork must come down first. I think four taking the old place down and six excavating at the new site would be the best plan. Will heads of gangs come down and see me in the morning about it please?"

"Yes, Sar," replied Chief.

Doctor then gave a further short discussion with the aid of his blackboard of the most practicable type of seat for their lavatories which consisted of a wooden box placed on top of the drums.

"Now with regard to the feeding of the children. It will have to start right away."

"May says she can't take anyone. She's got three going to school and a baby. I reckon she's got just as much as she can do," said Joe.

"It's just as easy to cook for four as it is for three. All you have to do is give them a dish of potatoes and tell them to sit down and eat it," replied padre.

"And you must all make them eat their food in your house otherwise they will take the stuff home and their parents will get it. We can't have that. It is the parents' fault that they run short of potatoes every year, not the child's. I do admit it is a very difficult problem but if anyone on the island can think of a better idea, I should be pleased to hear about it. Is there anything else?" asked the doctor.

"Nothing that I can think of, Sar," said Chief.

"Me neither," came the chorus.

"Well good night everyone."

"Good night, Sar," said the smiling chorus.

THE TRISTAN TIMES

☩ for Peace

V for Victory

Tristan da. Cunha   South Atlantic Ocean

No. 1.   Sat., 6th March, 1943.   **Price:** 3 Cigarettes or 4 big Potatoes.

FOREIGN NEWS.

Sun. 28th. The loss of a Corvette commanded by Lieutenant Seligman, R.N.R. is announced. Mr. Seligman visited Tristan da Cunha in his 300 ton barquentine "Capillar" in 1937.

There is fierce fighting in Southern Russia.

Mon. 1st. The R.A.F. dropped 1,000 tons of bombs on St. Nazaire in 30 minutes. 5 planes are missing. Western Germany was also bombed.

Tues. 2nd. The R.A.F. made the heaviest attack of the war on Berlin. Fires were seen 200 miles away. We lost 19 bombers.

Russians captured Demyansk in North Russia. There was a lot of fighting in Tunisia. The Allies shot down 30 axis planes for the loss of 5 of our planes.

Wed. 3rd. Berlin still burning. R.A.F. attacks on trains in Germany. One squadron alone destroyed 16 trains.

Russians captured Rzhev, which Hitler once said was worth half Berlin.

Thur. 4th. Allied forces in the south west Pacific wiped out a Japanese force of 12 transport ships, 10 warships and 55 airplanes. There were 15,000 Japanese soldiers in these ships, as well as the ships' crews. We lost 3 aircraft only in this battle.

R.A.F. made a heavy raid on Hamburg. Mines in Norway were also blown up. The Germans sent 40 or 50 machines to bomb London and lost 4 machines. Messina was bombed by American planes. U.S. planes bombed Rotterdam and Hamm. British submarines have sunk for certain 7 axis ships in the Mediterranean Sea in the last week.

Fri. 5th. Russians advancing south west of Rzhev.

CHURCH NOTICES.

Ash Wednesday H.C. at 7.15 a.m. Special Lent addresses each Wed. & Fri. 7 to 7.30 p.m. Other Services as usual.

Sat. 6th. The R.A.F. made a very heavy raid on Essen. We lost 14 bombers. Naples was bombed by aircraft operating from the Middle East. Gafsa in Tunisia is now surrounded on 2 sides by Allied forces.

Last month U.S. shipyards delivered 130 merchant ships, 150 warships, 700 landing barges and 1,460 naval aircraft.

ISLAND NEWS.

Sun. 28th. Six island boats returned from Nightingale Island with guano.

Wed. 3rd. A council meeting was held at 8.30 p.m. All 11 councillors were present, also the M.O.i/C. assisted by the Padre. It was decided that:-

1) School for the children would be started in the near future.

2) An A.R.P. practice for the islanders will be held on Tuesday at 2.30 p.m. so that they would know what to do if an enemy ship arrived at the island.

3) A deep-pit type of w.c. will soon be installed at every house.

4) From 1st May next each family will be allowed to keep 3 geese only.

5) Children must stop joking about "Sailo". There have been far too many false reports about ships.

6) Councillors may "hammer" any children they hear swearing.

7) Chief is asked to get together a small army of 12 islanders who will be issued with rifles.

8) No further word has been heard from the Colonial Office about the introduction of money at the island. The chit system of pay will continue.

9) Some men have agreed to put sheep up on the Base, where there is good pasturage.

10) Dr. Woolley issued a warning that dogs out at night will be shot.

Wed. 3rd. Johnnie Repetto's gang volunteered for work erecting 15 poles for the Church electric lighting, and by midday this was finished. Tom Rogers and "Big" Charlie Green did carpentry repairs to the Church.

Thur. 4th.
The Waterspout, as seen from the Met. Station at 8.50 am to-day.

The "TRISTAN TIMES" is registered by the M.O.i/C. as a Newspaper. Editor: A.B.Crawford. Foreign News: Dr. Woolley. Printed at "Martha's"

"The Tristan Times"

Tristan da Cunha has, at times in the past, had to wait as long as two or three years at a stretch without any news whatsoever from the 'outside world'. With the advent of the steamship and modern refrigeration methods of storing foodstuffs, ships no longer called there as they did in the past for fresh water and meat. In the days of sail one would see a dozen or so whalers on their way to or from the Antarctic, anchored off the island at one time, and those were happy and prosperous days for the twelve families that inhabited the island then. Since the close of the nineteenth century they considered themselves lucky if they saw a ship once in a year.

World War II brought something fresh for Tristan, a wireless station with radios of the latest design which kept islanders and military personnel up to date with the latest war news throughout our stay.

The idea to publish a weekly newspaper first came to me in January 1942 before I even left Cape Town for Tristan to take part in the building of the military establishment there. Even the type of heading I would use was designed in the Cape long before I set foot on the island later on in the year. But when I eventually arrived the chaos of building, which lasted for fully 8 months, gave me little inducement to take up the pen of journalism.

It was not until 6 March 1943, almost a year after our arrival, that I was able to work up the enthusiasm required and the Naval officer in charge, Dr Woolley, kindly offered to join the 'staff' as Foreign Correspondent. That made the staff of two with me as editor and publisher. It was decided that the original idea of calling the paper *The Tristan Times* after the famous London newspaper, *The Times*, should be adhered to, although for military reasons we were not able to write to the editor of *The Times* for permission to do so!

In order that the paper should have official status, it should be copyright and registered like all proper newspapers; it was necessary to put it onto a sound financial basis, otherwise it might be argued that it was nothing more than a circular or a magazine. But here the difficulty arose on account of the absence of any currency on the island, for the local population have never used any money and the sailors bought goods at the naval canteen on the 'tick' system, the position of their financial status being radioed to the Cape at the end of each month. In the absence of money, how were we going to charge people for their weekly news?

A Tristan's wealth is measured by the quantity of potatoes he possessed in his bins at the end of the 'digging' season, and potatoes were often used locally for barter and exchange. It was therefore decided that the islanders should buy their papers in potatoes and the sailors, well, every sailor carried one thing common almost to them all in his pocket, they would buy them with cigarettes. With the paper now placed on a 'financial' basis, production proceeded and on 6 March 1943 the first copy of the *Tristan Times* appeared on the island, their first newspaper.

Every single day of the week for the next thirty weeks, Dr Woolley listened in to the wireless in his office to the B.B.C. news broadcasts and, in a special diary for the purpose, kept records of the weekly overseas news. Every Saturday morning, likewise without fail, we would hold a 'press conference' in his office when I would make notes from his diary at his dictation and edit the material into readable form suitable for our small newspaper. From about five or six o'clock on Saturday afternoons until sometimes one or two o'clock on Sunday mornings I used to edit, publish and print the *Tristan Times* up at the house of Arthur and Martha Rogers.

The paper was printed on one side of a piece of foolscap paper, being roneod on two machines, one quarto size for the heading, which always remained the same, and the other on the office foolscap size machine, onto which were typed the items of island and international news. This one varied from week to week, the actual printing process being two separate operations, hand operated of course. The paper was divided into two columns with usually the whole of the left hand side devoted to wireless news, mostly war news in those days, and the right hand side local or island news.

It was decided that the newspaper was worth three cigarettes per copy for the naval personnel and the first idea was that the islanders would buy theirs for one pound of potatoes a copy each week. The difficulty carrying a set of scales from house to house on which to measure the islanders' purchase price was soon obvious, and it was decided in those autumnal days of plenty that this idea should be replaced by four big potatoes a copy. This held and was well received locally for the first three weeks. As the winter wore on, however, the value of this commodity rose as the islanders ate up their potatoes, and four big potatoes was soon replaced by four potatoes per copy. By the month of May this price had to be further reduced to three, and eventually, by 7 July when some of the less industrious islanders had but few potatoes left in their bins, the price reached its lowest figure of two potatoes per copy, at which it remained. The price to the sailors of three cigarettes did not alter.

When after church *The Tristan Times* was ready for sale on Sunday mornings, two news vendors, Harold Green and Lindsay Repetto, each about eight years of age, would come running up to the house where I lived for their twenty copies a piece, for the islanders usually purchased exactly forty copies per week, which wasn't bad out of a total population of fifty-two families. With small 'gunny' bags or sacks slung over their shoulders, off they would go from house to house to see who could finish first, the requisite number of potatoes being deposited into the sacks by each housewife. As payment for their work Harold and Lindsay received sweets, lump sugar and biscuits which I was able to purchase at the naval canteen.

I distributed the twenty-five copies down at the naval station myself after divisions and filled my pockets with their seventy-five cigarettes, sometimes with the utmost difficulty, for they were always keen to get their papers and the money was showered at me faster than I could cope with it. Most of the sailors insisted on collecting complete sets and those who lost back numbers used to try to have them replaced.

The *The Tristan Times* presented quite an interesting record of World War II from the forcing of the Mareth line, through the Sicilian campaign right up till the capitulation of Italy and the abdication of the Italian monarch. On the other hand, reading the right hand column, the island news, gave a good idea as to what was going on on the island throughout that period. The most popular items of island news recorded were birthdays, reports of council meetings, the activities of the T.D.V. (local home guard) and church notices close runners up.

An interesting item of news announced on Saturday, 3 July, 1943 foretold of the then imminent Sicilian and Italian campaign and read as follows:

England: Mr. Churchill, speaking in London after receiving the Freedom of the City, stated that there will be heavy fighting in the Mediterranean and elsewhere before the leaves of autumn fall. We must be prepared to face sacrifices.

An attempt was made in the publishing of the news in the paper to compromise between setting the material out in simple language so that the islanders, who have little idea of the modern world, would be able to take an intelligent interest in what was going on, and at the same time maintain a sufficiently high standard for the naval ratings. Slang words, unknown to the former, were kept out altogether and Dr Woolley and I tried to maintain the dignity of our weekly by eliminating altogether second rate wisecracks and jokes directed against other members of the station.

During the history of the paper two free supplements were published. The first, on 17 April, 1943, was a map of the world on which the small island of Tristan da Cunha was prominently marked and was intended to show the islanders which countries were on the Allied side and who were the Axis. Supplement No. 2 was issued free, on the 1 August, on the occasion of the Editor's birthday and consisted of a large scale map of the island showing the more important geographical names, including beaches, gulches and other prominent landmarks. This supplement was particularly well received down at the Naval Station.

There were two stop press announcements, the first on the occasion of a ship bound for the middle east with military equipment passed the island after midnight one Saturday night just after the *The Tristan Times* had gone to press. It was not too late, however, to be included as a stop press notice on the outside of all copies printed. The second also concerned a ship, this time a ship bound for the island from the Cape with stores and mail.

There was panic in the printing world when the letter R of the printer's typewriter broke out of commission, and Leading/Tel. Fletcher kindly put his deft fingers to work and with the aid of a portion of a darning needle put the machine back into operation.

It has often been asked what happened to the payment which resulted from the sale of the papers. If in those days I had known of the shortage of potatoes in South Africa and the scarcity of cigarettes in England, we might have made some special arrangements and short of a more honourable negotiation become quite well-to-do on the black market but our ultimate disposal of our profits was more law-abiding. As family man, Dr Woolley had his wife and three children with him on the island, it seemed the obvious solution was to present him with the potatoes as his 'pay' for the chair of 'foreign news editor' and, with regard to the cigarettes, I was a smoker in those days and I suppose they just went the way of all cigarettes.

Many copies of the *The Tristan Times* were illustrated with maps showing the progress of the war, especially in North Africa and Italy. It is rather strange that the very first item of foreign news ever collected by Dr Woolley on the very first day reported the loss of a corvette commanded by Lieutenant Seligman, R.N.R. 'Mr Seligman,' the news went on, 'visited Tristan da Cunha in his three hundred ton barquentine *Cap Pilar* in 1937'. That was the only time we ever heard the name of the island mentioned, and it is strange that it should have been our first news item. Issue no. 1 of *The Tristan Times* also included a drawing of a waterspout observed off the island that same week.

Shortly before money was introduced onto the island, just after my departure, the sum of one halfpenny was added to the price of the paper, the final price when I left being: three cigarettes, two potatoes or a halfpenny per copy.

Reports of council meetings given in the paper showed the island potato crop for the season 1942-43 to be 4,429 bushels, which represented an average of 85 bushels per family. Seeing that some families reaped something like one hundred and fifty bushels for themselves, it was at once evident that others, the lazy islanders, must have had no more than twenty to thirty bushels to last them over the twelve months until the following year's crops were recorded. This at once showed that there were industrious and lazy islanders, or to be very polite, good and bad farmers. The families of these 'poor' people were half-starved towards the middle of the winter when the bins were empty, which resulted in the following report in the *The Tristan Times* of Saturday 21st August 1943:

> *Monday 16th. A Council Meeting was held in the evening, all councillors being present. Dr Woolley informed them that islanders who are short of potatoes already have been ordered to put in more ground. The feeding of children of the poorer families will also have to be started shortly.*

Tristan newsvendors: Lindsay Repetto and
Harold Green about to set out one Sunday
morning to deliver *The Tristan Times* with sacks
in which to collect potatoes in payment.

The Tristan Defence Volunteers

Tristan da Cunha was like many other remote spots, not excluded from activity and upheaval as the result of World War II, for throughout most of the time the South Atlantic was classed as a danger zone. From the time the *Graf Spee* was sunk in the mouth of the River Plate until the invasion of Europe by the Allies in 1944, enemy submarines and raiders were known to be operating in the waters around the Cape and at one time the German raider *Stier* put into Gough Island, 250 miles south-south east of Tristan da Cunha for repairs.

Tristan da Cunha was as important to weather forecasting in Southern Africa as Greenland or Iceland was to the whole of Europe and it therefore played a vital part in the general war effort in spite of the isolation, although no actual fighting was experienced.

On Saturday 18 September 1943, the following item appeared in *The Tristan Times*:

> *ISLAND NEWS*.
>
> *On Tuesday 14th, early in the afternoon, a ship appeared unexpectedly coming from the Eastward. The possibility existed of her belonging to an enemy power as the Medical Officer-in-Charge had received no signal from Naval Headquarters in the Cape of any ship's arrival due on that day. An alarm was therefore sounded at the Naval Station and both the station active defence unit and the local TRISTAN DEFENCE VOLUNTEERS took up positions with rifles, machine guns and hand grenades in the event of anything untoward happening. The civilian population automatically and most efficiently evacuated to Hottentot Gulch. After a while communication was established between ship and shore and she proved to be the American ship WILLIAM L DAVIDSON (Liberty type) whose captain had decided to put into Tristan da Cunha in urgent need of provisions. Although there was a strong wind blowing our boats put out to her with food enough to last 70 men for ten days and she sailed for South America shortly after midnight.*

On the following day after the excitement had died down, Surgeon Lieutenant-Commander E J S Woolley, O.B.E., R.N.V.R. told me he was glad that after eighteen months of isolation and very little real danger or excitement of this nature, we had at last been of some use to somebody, for at the time we did not appreciate fully the value of our weather reports to forecasting elsewhere. To think that we had possibly saved life by supplying much needed food to the crew of a ship was some consolation to us in our isolation.

These American sailors had been existing on a meagre ration of diluted pea soup for the past week and the prospects of a further ten days on this unattractive diet had prompted the captain to call at the world's loneliest island quite unaware of our existence there!

Although the enemy did not know it, the sum total of the defences of lonely Tristan da Cunha during World War II consisted of four pre-Great War Lewis machine guns, about two dozen .303 rifles and a few boxes of hand grenades! Once the Lewis guns were manned, by S.A.A.F. Meteorologists and Naval wireless telegraph operators, there was no one left to use the rifles, with the exception of non-coms such as the Doctor, the Padre, the cook and Naval nursing sister.

If the enemy were to attempt a landing it would have been a pity not to have made the best use of what little extra equipment we possessed. At the recommendation, therefore, of the then Commander W A Bishop, O.B.E., R.N., the officer in Simonstown who was largely responsible for the establishment of the Naval Station on the island, a local home guard was formed consisting of some of the more agile of the sixty adult male inhabitants on the island.

At a council meeting, on the 3 March 1943, at which the Doctor, Padre and I were present, the islanders agreed to form a home guard and Chief Willie Repetto their leader was asked to get together a dozen or so men and present the names to the Doctor the following week. Woolley asked me to be responsible for the formation of this unusual army, which came into being on the 17 April of that year.

On this day after Willie Repetto's sixteen men had reported to me for duty, each man was issued with a rifle, forty rounds of ammunition, a bayonet,

Sgt Hudson gives small arms instruction to the TDV

a steel helmet and webbing equipment. The men were proud indeed as they walked back to their thatched island homes bearing their newly acquired battle equipment which they kept at their bedsides ready for an emergency until the war came to an end.

It was decided to call this home guard the Tristan Defence Volunteers, a title which was soon shortened into the more popular form of the T.D.V.. Before it was possible to create a small army such as this it is first necessary to draw up a constitution, presenting to its members in simple language the conditions of service, so that when they sign on, they will then know their duties and responsibilities. I therefore had to draw up a constitution and at a special parade which was held in one of the island homes, the ten articles of the constitution of the T.D.V. were read to them amidst great interest. Article 3 read as follows:

> *The object of the T.D.V. is firstly to support the naval active defence unit in preventing an enemy landing at the island, and secondly to defend their homes, women and children in the Settlement in the event of the naval unit being overwhelmed and the enemy succeeding in getting ashore.*

Having created a little army of just sixteen men, consisting of eleven married and five young bachelors, it was necessary to give them instructions so that they would know what to do in the event of an emergency. Thereupon the T.D.V. was formed into two sections known as the Eastward and the Westward sections, each being placed under the command of a sergeant and a corporal, both islanders.

Sergeant Arthur Rogers, whose forefather came from the United States of America, and Corporal Johnnie Repetto were responsible for the westward Section. Sergeant Arthur Repetto, whose father was an Italian sailor cast away on the island in 1892 and Corporal John the Baptist Lavarello were in charge of the eastward section. I need hardly mention that the eight men of each section lived in the corresponding area of the Settlement of their section designation.

White linen armbands with the letters T.D.V. stencilled in black were issued to each man, and later on the N.C.O.s were sent brass chevrons specially manufactured for them in the Cape of Good Hope.

In order to bring these men up to maximum efficiency it was necessary to hold parades every week and, with the valuable assistance of Corporals H J Heighway of Kimberley and D G Hudson of Durban of the South African Air Force Meteorological Service, the islanders were instructed in the care and maintenance of the rifle, the firing of a machine gun, the throwing of hand grenades and various other military escapades. Apart from the fact that one or two islanders already possessed .303 rifles for the shooting of sea elephants and

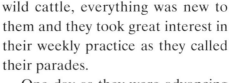

Meteorologists and three telegraphists inspect a World War One Lewis gun, the most modern means of defence while a meteorologist demonstrates the launching of a hand-grenade to members of the TDV.

wild cattle, everything was new to them and they took great interest in their weekly practice as they called their parades.

One day as they were advancing in line formation over the island plateau jumping behind rocks and sniping at imaginary enemy landing troops, one man was heard to say in great enthusiasm: 'I guess them Garmans would get no farver than Big Watron afore they'd all be dead!', whereupon another, with a wink in his eye and a good-natured jibe at the expense of their crack shooter, Ned Green, put in the joyful reminder that if 'Ned had got his old form back, I sure reckon they'd never even reach Big Beach, let alone Big Watron!'

But their most popular weekly parades were their shooting matches and many happy hours were spent out on the Hottentot Point rifle range, which was especially constructed for this purpose on the edge of the plateau. Missed shots, and there were many during the first few weeks, harmlessly dropped into the sea and did no more damage than threaten whales and porpoises. The targets consisted of the circular tops of petrol drums mounted on blue-gum poles which had been used for the building of the naval establishment. The discs were painted black and white with bulls, inner and outer circles. We had our own method of scoring with bulls counting six, inners five and outers four. Each person was allowed ten rounds of ammunition, the maximum score therefore at each shoot being sixty points per man.

The first shooting practice for the raw Tristan Defence Volunteers was held on the 14 April and the islanders were so nervous that out of the thirteen persons who tried to make names for themselves as marksmen four never hit the target at all and six others scored less than ten points out of a possible sixty! The average score for the day was only 6.4 points per man, and we prayed that no enemy would attempt a landing at this stage, otherwise our very existence was at stake with the odds greatly against our survival!

As time went on, however, our warriors gradually gained confidence as first one and then another put up a good show.

"I sure ain't going to let Fred beat me h'every time," said Arthur Rogers one day after putting up a magnificent score of forty.

But Fred Swain kept his lead with a forty-one the following week. It was in this good-spirited manner that the islanders improved week by week, until 5 August when they considered themselves fit to challenge the Royal Navy to a match.

This great event took place on the same range. Sergeants Arthur Rogers and Arthur Repetto each selected a team of six men, whereas Dr Woolley and Corporal Hudson produced equal sized teams consisting of Naval ratings of various ranks.

Before the match started the Doctor generously offered a packet of twenty cigarettes to the six men in the winning team, opening the score for his own side with a useful forty-two. After a keenly contested event the count at the end of the day showed Islander Arthur Roger's team the victors by one point, his men scoring 173 against Corporal Hudson whose team scored 172. On the other hand the Royal Navy as a whole beat the combined T.D.V. score for the day; but the islanders were very proud when they walked off with the cigarettes, for sometimes they go for several months or even years without a single smoke. If the enemy had attempted a landing the T.D.V. would have fought like wild dogs!

One of the most interesting incidents in the history of the T.D.V. was the manner in which official recognition was acquired without a direct approach on the subject being placed before the Naval Authorities in the Cape. Often enough a direct approach resulted in delay and instead of complying with our humble request we were apt to have our enthusiasm dampened by our superiors, often for all time.

I wanted the T.D.V. properly recognised and as I had carefully kept three copies of all correspondence in connection with the formation of this institution, I presented them with a fait accompli upon my return to the Cape and lent them the file. The good gentlemen of the navy were most interested and my fears were allayed, but, and a very big BUT, I had made a gross mistake in the eyes of International Law in the wording of the Certificate of Membership which was given to each islander.

These certificates were signed by Dr Woolley as Medical Officer-in-Charge and Magistrate of the island and contained the following words:

> *...in all matters of Training and Operations against the enemy, you will carry out such instructions and Orders as may be given by me and any N.C.O. to whom I delegate the Authority.*

They quite rightly maintained that, 'A Medical Officer, as a non-combatant, is not entitled in the eyes of International Law to give instructions of a military nature' Accordingly, they issued new certificates almost identical with my originals, except for a change in that vital wording, drawn up and sent back to the island for redistribution to the 16 men of the T.D.V.

Although I was a little disappointed that my original certificates were withdrawn, it was really one of the best things that could have happened, as their taking exception to the original wording showed without question that they accepted the organisation and their action in issuing new certificates was in itself a confirmation of their recognition.

If Mr Winston Churchill's suggestion of the Allied Nations striking a Victory Medal bears fruit, an effort will be made to have this medal granted to the sixteen men of the T.D.V. whose rifles constituted a major portion of the island defence system. I have been informed that they were on the same footing as other Colonial troops who were not actually in a fighting area during the war, but who will be entitled to such an award if one is instituted at a later date.

The islanders thoroughly enjoyed their parades and always behaved well. If the enemy had attempted a landing they would have fought to the last, as was displayed by their general enthusiasm and by their conduct on the occasion of the arrival of the unidentified ship. It was almost the real thing and their fingers were ready and guns cocked until the Doctor sent a note by runner to say that she was a friendly American ship. Each man relaxed, and took his finger off the trigger.

Tristan da Cunha Mails

Tristan da Cunha was probably the only community of English speaking people in the world who have no postage stamps or proper postal facilities and the history of letters posted at the island is an interesting study in itself.

At intervals, perhaps every one or two years, the premeditated visit of a ship allows incoming mails to be received, and the departure of such a ship, or of any other vessel that may happen to call, gave the inhabitants the chance of dispatching an outgoing mail. As there was no postal administration, all out going mail is considered as 'Paquebot' and letters posted on board the ship taking them away were franked with the stamps of the country under whose flag the vessel sailed.

In practice, however, as the islanders have no money to buy stamps from the ship, letters either bore no stamps at all or they had British stamps which might have been sent from Britain by friends of the community or were in possession of the resident missionary.

Unstamped letters were sometimes charged on delivery in their country of destination at the single rate of 'postage due', but kindly postmasters often delivered them free, examples, perhaps the only one, of a compassionate mail! Although they had no stamps, the islanders provided themselves years ago with a postmark and impressed this on their outgoing mail, either upon the stamp or upon the envelope. It has not been ascertained when this was first used, but it was probably, towards the end of the last century.

This mark, Type 1, is a small one and consists of the name of the island enclosed within a double-lined circle.

From 1886 to 1900, the year after the terrible life-boat disaster of 1885, the Admiralty had been accustomed to send a warship annually to the island from Simonstown but this practice was discontinued and the island was without an official visit until that of *H.M.S. Dublin* in 1923. During the intervening twenty odd years the island had only occasional chance visits from merchant vessels.

Type 2 postmark, the die to which was made to the order of Mr Percy Creaghe, was sent to the island by him in March 1919, and was first seen on a mail brought off by *H.M.S. Yarmouth* on 1 August of that year. That mark remained in use until 1929, but was not the only one employed during those ten years. It was a large heavy mark of real post office type. Most marks were in violet, a few in a light greyish or brownish black.

In 1922 a fresh type of postmark, Type 3, was brought into use, a 'missionary' mark with a Maltese cross on it, presumably taken there by the Rev. Rogers who landed in April of that year.

During the next three years Type 2 and Type 3 were used. In May 1922 the *R.Y.S. Quest*, the ship of the Shackleton-Rowett Antarctic Expedition, called and took off mails.

In 1927 Tristan came into the limelight by becoming a place of call for tourist ships and a cover brought from Tristan proves this by the letter inside, which was written on Tristan in May 1926, although the cover itself had only the mark '*R.M.P.S.P. Asturias* posted on the high seas 19 Feb 1927' and the London paquebot cancellation of March 14 1927. In 1928 a new postmark, Type 4, first appeared, this was recorded with a handwritten date added. This was larger than the Type 3 mark and the Maltese cross is replaced by a five-pointed star.

A cover with a Cape Town paquebot cancellation, dated 24 February 1934, with no stamps, had in the letter inside the statement 'We have no stamper on Tristan, so I can only write Tristan da Cunha', which was written on the envelope. This letter was taxed 2d. on arrival in England.

A cover of later in the year, however, marked as received in London on 22 October 1934, has a mark which I call Type 5. This is very similar to Type 3, but was slightly smaller and the space between the Maltese cross and the beginning and end of 'Tristan da Cunha' was definitely smaller than in the Type 3 mark.

The island was visited by *H.M.S. Carlisle* at the beginning of March 1937, and covers with King Edward VIII stamps came back by it. The ship itself had a special souvenir envelope for the occasion, reference to which will be found in the South African Philatelist, of August 1937. The covers coming by the *Carlisle*, although the Type 5 Tristan mark was present, the stamps were not as a rule cancelled by it. They received Cape Town or London Paquebot cancellations. Finally, on 22 January 1938, delivered in Johannesburg, there arrived a mail with covers bearing King Edward VIII stamps and King George VI stamps, this time the stamps were cancelled by the Tristan Type 5 mark.

During the early part of World War II, 1939-1942, the Type 5 mark was in operation. On the 5 April 1942, when we arrived on the island, Tristan became a danger zone and a military area. A system of censorship therefore had to be introduced, not only for the military and naval personnel, but also for the islanders, for if the news leaked out that we were using the island for strategic purposes, a German raider or submarine might have lost no time in wiping us off the map, or at any rate attempting to do so!

The Type 5 mark was therefore withdrawn altogether by Dr Woolley, the the officer-in-charge and chief authority on the island. The military and naval personnel mail was all marked 'On Active Service', censored and marked with the usual naval censor stamp initialled and dated by Dr Woolley. No stamps were necessary, as was usual for members of His Majesty's Forces.

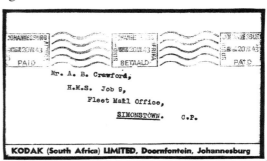

Addressed to the author at his secret wartime address at HMS Job 9

The question then arose as to how the island mail should be dealt with, as the use of the Type 5 mark on letters in the same mailbag as 'On Service' letters would give the game away should the ship bearing them be captured and her papers examined. It was therefore decided that the name Tristan, in any shape or form, should not be allowed to appear either in the text or on the covers of both military and civilian mail leaving the island throughout the war. The civilian mail, in which there was often less than a dozen or so letters in those days, was treated in the same way, with the exception of the wording 'On Service' which was omitted altogether.

Tristan letters therefore, although bearing nothing more than the address and naval censor marks, were carried free throughout the latter part of the war and there is no record of any postage due rates having been charged on delivery. Both military and civilian mail was placed in proper mail bags or sacks and handed to the captains of passing ships no matter in which direction he was proceeding. He was asked to give the sack, however, to the port authorities, naval authorities or postal authorities in his first port of call for forwarding on to England and South Africa.

It was a matter of conjecture, for me at the time, as to what happened to the letters after this. Some were marked with circular and rectangular paquebot marks, although bearing already the naval censorship stamp. Others on the other hand were not touched with paquebot at all, and I have on record one letter that came through from the island in quite a different manner. Anxious to see what would happen to a letter posted on board a passing ship without the islander submitting the letter locally for censoring, I asked one of my best and most trustworthy island friends to hand the letter to the sailor of a passing ship, a commission which he most faithfully accomplished. It appeared that the sailor added the words 'On Service' and placed it in the ship's mail letter box. It then took the ordinary course of military mail and received paquebot cancellations and was delivered to me successfully in Pretoria.

Addressed to the author after leaving the island with the Naval censure cachet but no indication of the sender

The correct address of the island had never been laid down, but would appear to be 'Tristan da Cunha, South Atlantic Ocean'. Mails to the island, however were so rare that, when they did occur, the Admiralty or shipping authorities notified the postal people of the latest date for posting and the Postmaster General usually arranged for a notice to be published in the press, sometimes giving special instructions such as: *The address to be used is as follows; Tristan da Cunha, via G.P.O., London*, or such like. Alternatively, it might be *via Cape Town* but letters from South Africa to the island were usually just addressed *Tristan da Cunha, South Atlantic* or merely bore the name of the island.

Here World War II presented another difficulty, letters could not be addressed to soldiers and sailors as Tristan da Cunha for not only was their station a secret and unknown by their relatives but a ship intercepted bearing such mail in the South Atlantic would at once give away the game that Tristan was of military importance, with possible drastic action resulting from the enemy.

From the day we landed in 1942, therefore, until the end of 1943, the address used by our relatives was, in recognition of the scheme's secret name *H.M.S. 'Job 9' c/o Fleet Mail Office, Cape Town, S. Africa.*

These letters were of course collected at the G.P.O. Cape Town and delivered to the naval Fleet Mail Office in the Docks. They were kept until the Admiral's Office ordered them to be placed aboard certain ships, which were proceeding with stores to the island on a given date. In the past the islanders had considered themselves lucky if they got a mail once in two years but on average they were enabled to dispatch mail at least once in twelve months. Sometimes, however several years elapsed before they could either receive or dispatch letters and those were hard days for the isolated population.

The establishment of meteorological and wireless stations there and the placing of personnel from England and the Cape meant regular supplies of provisions being sent and we used to see a ship at least once every four months. As the progress of the war turned more in favour of the Allied powers, the diminishing number of enemy shipping gave less cause for secrecy and from the 1 January 1944 the address of personnel on the island changed. The sailors were now stationed on *H.M.S. Atlantic Isle* and this replaced *H.M.S. Job 9* in the address given above.

The meteorological station relief team (*) handover: Crawford, Hurford*, Heighway, Schoeman*, Dyer* and Hudson.

The launching of *HMS Atlantic Isle*, the island now being designated a shore establishment.
(*courtesy Ron Burn*)

Homeward Bound

hy was it necessary to disturb the Tristan da Cunha community in wartime when they could have been left in peace? It was the very isolation of the place that was so vital for the Allied cause. Not as a fortress, for we had no guns or fortifications installed there, but it was used as a listening post for enemy raiders and submarines when they surfaced to transmit their daily radio messages to their headquarters in their homelands. Not only did our naval communicators retransmit their messages to the Admiralty in Britain, but they also revealed the direction and positions of the enemy ships. Such information was of course vital, but there were other advantages.

Just as all wartime operations, whether military, naval or aviation were dependent on the weather, daily weather reports from Tristan, in the middle of the South Atlantic Ocean, were of great value. These reports however had to be re-coded so that the enemy could not benefit from the information. That was why we three Air Force meteorologists spent eighteen months on the station. All weather forecasting throughout the world was based on daily weather charts. We did not need to plot these on Tristan, but they were very useful elsewhere, especially for shipping forecasts.

By 14 October 1943 our time had come to an end and we were replaced by three more weather men from South Africa who arrived in time for special instructions in the vagaries of Tristan's fierce gales, which were influenced by the infamous 'Roaring Forties', sometimes of hurricane force.

We reluctantly bid our final adieus to our islander friends. The ship designated to pick us up on the 14th of the month was the Shell tanker *Tornus*, bound from the west to the Middle East with high octane oil on board via CapeTown.

For our services we were awarded the appropriate World War II, Defence, Victory and Africa Service Medals.

Epilogue

A brief summary of developments on Tristan da Gunha since World War II might be welcome since literature on the subject is often not abundant.

The welfare of the present community, which has reached some 300 souls, is in good hands and is normally of a higher standard. As the result of the closure of the Naval station at the end of hostilities in 1946, and a scientific enquiry, currency had been introduced and by 1949 a local crawfish processing factory was established. The product is exported to dollar earning countries like the United States.

A small boat harbour was constructed close to the Settlement, the company operating the licence being established in Cape Town, the nearest port. In order to control all this new development, the British Government in London appointed an Administrator, under the nominal jurisdiction of the Governor of St. Helena, who visits his outpost once a year in January to 'show the Flag'. Meanwhile, a post office was opened on the island and postage stamps introduced.

An island school was built to accommodate about thirty pupils, staffed by teachers trained in St. Helena and the United Kingdom. The policy was to educate the islanders to such a standard that they eventually would be able to replace as many expatriots as possible – to save expense.

Local government is by a dozen elected councillors, under the chairmanship of the Administrator who holds magisterial powers over the community. Among other things, they pass bye-laws which protect local wildlife, concerning bird and fishing sanctuaries, rock lobster, seals and whales.

Like the Administrator, a qualified doctor is appointed for one or two year periods who operates from the local well-equipped Camogli Hospital, which is staffed by local nurses, islanders trained in St. Helena. The doctor has available a modern seaworthy rescue vessel enabling him to execute emergency first aid to the crews of passing vessels when required.

The old naval canteen has now been turned into a supermarket, supplied from the Cape, for islanders who operate gas stoves, videos, refrigerators and modern technology. We hear that they now possess over fifty motor vehicles on the island in place of the bullock carts, donkeys and Shanks' ponies which kept them strong and healthy in days gone by.

Likewise appointed from the Cape of Good Hope is a resident clergyman for the Anglican Church and a small chapel run by islanders caters for the Catholics.

Queen's Day is celebrated as a public holiday every summer and a fine day once or twice a year is selected as Ratting Day, when teams of islanders compete with dogs to exterminate the rats, that otherwise eat the potato crops.

The island hit world headlines in 1961 when the 'extinct' volcano unexpectedly burst into activity, and the whole population had to be evacuated to the United Kingdom for safety. After two years of civilization in the modern world, 90% returned to the tranquillity of their old island homes.

A severe hurricane in May 2001, which caused many thousands of pounds damage, has not caused them to dampen their desire to remain in, what to them is, the 'best place on earth'.

Allan Crawford

March 2004
Wadhurst, East Sussex

Observation spot on Herald Point

Index